C000264099

THE PATH IS THE WAY

TO SELF-MASTERY
Guide

Frederick A. Martinez

Copyright © 2024 by Frederick A. Martinez

All rights reserved. No part of this book may be used or reproduced in any form whatsoever without written permission except in the case of brief quotations in critical articles or reviews.

Printed in the United States of America.
Book design by (Frederick A. Martinez)
Cover design by (Frederick A. Martinez)

ISBN – eBook: 978-1-962570-49-7
ISBN – Paperback: 978-1-962570-50-3
ISBN – Ingram Spark: 978-1-962570-51-0

First Edition: February 2024

For more information or to book an event, contact:
www.FredMartinez.info
www.ThePathIsTheWay.com

THE PATH IS THE WAY

TO SELF-MASTERY
Guide

Frederick A. Martinez

SPOTLIGHT
PUBLISHING HOUSE

Goodyear, Arizona

CONTENTS

INTRODUCTION

"Mastering others is strength.
Mastering yourself is true power."
—Lao Tzu

I am thrilled to embark on a journey to self-mastery with you! The path to self-mastery is an exciting and rewarding journey filled with opportunities for growth, learning, and personal transformation. This path requires courage, commitment, and a willingness to explore your deepest desires, values, and beliefs. As we walk this path together, we will discover the inner resources we possess and learn how to tap into our full potential to create a fulfilling, joyful, and meaningful life. So, thank you for taking this journey with me, and let's get started on the path to self-mastery!

Each subject is merely a checkpoint on your path to self-mastery. If you let life be your teacher, self-mastery is a continuous process of learning and growth. You are the only one who can decide when to move on to the next lesson. There will be difficulties in life, but do not be concerned—there are only pass-or-fail outcomes. Passing indicates advancement; however, failing allows you to get up and try again, this time with the knowledge gained from the first attempt.

The path to self-mastery will appear in its own mysterious and captivating way, seeking out those ready to embark on a profound journey of personal transformation. It is not a quest that can be forced or manipulated, for it possesses a pearl of inherent wisdom that guides individuals toward their destined awakening. As we navigate life, we often operate in one of two distinct modes: evading or pursuing certain aspects, depending on our circumstances. However, where this expedition begins holds little significance compared to the awe-inspiring transformation it promises.

Many internal demons follow us through the maze of self-discovery, silently nagging us to face the worries, uncertainties, and insecurities we've long tried to avoid. These demons can take on many guises, including self-doubt, limiting beliefs, and past traumas. They continually speak in our ears, affecting our choices and preventing us from reaching our full potential. The path to self-mastery offers a rare chance to engage in a ferocious battle with these inner demons and conquer them with unflinching courage and tenacity. Only until we muster the courage to face and conquer these shadows will we be able to break free from the chains that have shackled us and release the limitless power that exists inside.

It is now, at this precise instant, that we should begin this transforming conflict with our inner demons. We can no longer avoid them or try to get around their influence. Instead, we must face them head-on, not with hostility or violence, but with a loving resolve that strives to understand their cause and break their hold on our lives. Exploring the depths of our minds allows us to uncover the foundations of our fears and doubts, bringing them to the surface for analysis and eventual release. By removing the layers of self-imposed restrictions in this sacred confrontation, we liberate ourselves to explore our true potential fully.

The process of engaging with our internal demons requires great introspection and self-reflection. It demands an unwavering commitment to honesty and vulnerability as we navigate the intricate layers of our emotions, thoughts, and experiences. Yet, within this courageous confrontation lies the key to unlocking our authenticity and personal power. Through self-exploration, we discover the vast reservoirs of resilience, strength, and wisdom that have long resided within us, waiting to be harnessed and utilized for our growth.

Recognizing that the road to self-mastery is not a straight one free of obstacles is essential. It's a difficult journey with ups and downs, successes and failures. However, we develop and advance through these times of strife and conflict. With every demon vanquished, we surpass the limitations that have held us back, moving ever closer to a life of limitless freedom, meaning, and fulfillment.

As we travel along this transforming path, we understand that our journey—not our starting or end point—defines who we are. Instead, what counts most is how our efforts create a profound sense of self-mastery. Adopting this inspiring quest enables us to rewrite our own stories and create a masterpiece of our lives characterized by authenticity, passion, and unwavering growth.

Consequently, gather your strength and face the inner demons that have eluded you for far too long. Take part in the struggle that will free you from the self-imposed restrictions impeding your development. Take advantage of the transforming potential of self-mastery and embark on a journey of profound self-discovery to liberate your true potential and embrace the limitless opportunities ahead of you.

I will share a personal story of triumphing over a personal demon after a heartbreaking divorce. I started to surround myself with positive motivation and therapy. What I am about to share, I never told anybody. I stumbled upon a profound realization. It became painfully clear that I had relinquished my role as a leader in my relationship, allowing inauthenticity to seep into the very fabric of our connection. The consequence? A gradual erosion of respect that threatened to consume the love we once shared.

I was not able to express myself without the fear of judgment. Not able to express my wants, needs, and desires in the relationship. This caused me to create fantasies in my mind and look to the internet for an outlet. I can tell you from experience that this is unhealthy and not a way to live. It created unrealistic expectations; it decreased intimacy and emotional connection, causing communication breakdown, dissatisfaction, and addictive behaviors. It also rewires your brain, looking to get dopamine from each mouse click. You are being anchored like Pavlov's dog, experiencing arousal at the sound of the dinner bell, with or without the food in the bowl. The content producers know this and want to control you.

When you free yourself from this control, you are liberated, and it all starts by going on a life-changing journey toward self-mastery, where you will discover your incredible potential. It gives me great pleasure to accompany you on this enlightening journey of self-exploration, self-discovery, self-understanding, self-love, and self-transformation. So, get ready for a remarkable odyssey as we explore the depths of your being to uncover the magnificence that lies within.

Step 1: Self-Exploration - The Inner Expedition

Self-exploration is the first step on our journey to self-mastery. We will embark on an inner journey, leaving no stone unturned as we navigate the complex terrain of our thoughts, beliefs, and desires.

Together, we will investigate the core of who you are, your values, and the driving forces behind your actions. By peering into the depths of your soul, we will reveal the patterns that have shaped your life, both empowering and limiting. Through introspection and reflection, we will gain the clarity needed to ignite the spark of change.

Step 2: Self-Discovery - Unveiling Your True Potential

Self-discovery will unlock the doors to discover your unique gifts, talents, and passions. The process will unveil the hidden potential to be free through immersive exercises and soul-stirring conversations. You will uncover your creative potential beyond any boundaries you may have set for yourself. You will discover areas of strength and areas for improvement, guiding you toward genuine self-realization and contentment.

Step 3: Self-Understanding - Illuminating the Inner Landscape

Now, it's time to illuminate the inner landscape of your being. Self-understanding is the key that unlocks the secrets to your success and happiness. Together, we will delve into the depths of your emotions, fears, and aspirations, unraveling the intricate tapestry of your psyche. By dissecting your past experiences and examining the lessons they hold, we will gain valuable insights into the patterns that have shaped your life. Then, armed with this knowledge, we will rewrite the narratives that no longer serve you and create a blueprint for personal growth.

Step 4: Self-Love - Embracing Your Authentic Self

We will go on a voyage of self-love during this vital stage, accepting and embracing every facet of our true selves. We will cultivate a strong sense of compassion, understanding that your flaws are what make you unique. We shall mend old scars through forgiveness, gratitude, and opening doors to self-acceptance. Your confidence will soar due to developing a loving relationship with yourself, and you'll draw in the plenty waiting for you.

Step 5: Self-Transformation - Becoming the Architect of Your Destiny

Self-transformation is the last step on our path to self-mastery. You will now enter your true power armed with self-exploration, self-discovery, self-understanding, and self-love. By taking purposeful action, you will create a life that aligns with your highest desires and take control of your future. We'll put empowering tactics, routines, and rituals into place that move you closer to your objectives. You will understand that you are the most powerful change agent as you watch your transformation take place.

The journey toward self-mastery is a profound and thrilling adventure. You can realize your enormous potential through self-examination, self-discovery, self-understanding, self-love, and self-transformation. You can reshape your life and forge a purpose-filled future.

SELF-EXPLORATION

"To be yourself in a world that is constantly trying to make you something else is the greatest accomplishment."
—*Ralph Waldo Emerson*

Self-exploration is the foundation and the cornerstone of the path to self-mastery. In this chapter, we'll dive deep into the essence of who you are and what drives you. Self-exploration is about understanding yourself at a level you never thought possible. It's about identifying your values, strengths, weaknesses, passions, and limiting beliefs. It's about clarifying what makes you tick and what holds you back. And it's about using that knowledge to create a life aligned with your deepest desires and purpose.

But why is self-exploration so crucial in the journey to self-mastery? The answer is simple - it's impossible to master yourself without knowing yourself. You can only improve what you understand. You can only align your actions with your values if you know what they are. You can't overcome your limiting beliefs if you're unaware of them. And you can only pursue your passions and purpose if you know what they are.

That's why in this chapter, we'll explore the different facets of self-exploration and offer you practical tools and exercises to help you gain a deeper understanding of yourself. First, we'll start by identifying your values - the principles that guide your decisions and actions. Then, we'll assess your strengths and weaknesses, discover your passions, and overcome your limiting beliefs. These are the building blocks of self-mastery. By mastering them, you'll be well on your way to creating a fulfilling, purposeful life aligned with your true self.

So, my friends, get ready to embark on a journey of self-discovery that will transform your life. Let's dive in and uncover the essence of who you are - the essence of your greatness.

It's important to note that self-exploration is not a one-time event but a lifelong practice. As you grow and evolve, so too will your understanding of yourself. Continual self-exploration involves the ongoing discovery of oneself, one's personal growth, and a sense of oneself. It's about staying curious and open to new experiences and being willing to challenge your beliefs and assumptions.

Please approach self-exploration with an open mind and heart in this chapter. Be kind to yourself as you uncover new truths and be patient as you work through any challenges. Finally, remember that self-exploration is not about judging or criticizing yourself but rather about accepting yourself and using that acceptance to propel yourself forward.

Self-exploration is one of the most valuable investments you can make. By gaining a deeper understanding of yourself, you'll be better equipped to navigate the challenges and opportunities that come your way. As a result, you'll be more confident in your decisions and actions, and you'll be able to create a life that aligns with your true purpose.

Let's begin our journey of self-exploration. Let's uncover the essence of who you are and unleash your full potential.

Understanding Self-Exploration

You see, understanding yourself is the foundation of personal growth and development. By knowing who you are, what you stand for, and what drives you, you'll be better equipped to navigate life's challenges and create a life of purpose and fulfillment.

So, let's start by defining what we mean by self-exploration. At its core, self-exploration is gaining a deeper understanding of oneself. It involves asking questions, reflecting on your experiences, and gaining insights into your personality, values, beliefs, and behaviors. Self-exploration is about peeling back the layers of your identity and getting to the essence of who you are.

But why is self-exploration so important? Well, it allows you to gain a greater sense of self-awareness. When you understand your thoughts, feelings, and behaviors, you can see patterns and make connections you may not have noticed before. This self-awareness is the first step towards creating meaningful changes in your life.

In addition, identifying values through self-exploration assists in guiding principles that direct decisions and actions. When individuals know their values, they can align their life with them and make choices that are true to their inner selves, achieving more significant purpose and fulfillment.

Self-exploration also helps you to identify your strengths and weaknesses. When you know your strengths, you can leverage them to achieve your goals and make a meaningful impact. When you know your weaknesses, you can work on them and turn them into strengths. This self-awareness and personal development can lead to greater confidence and self-esteem.

So, how can you start your journey of self-exploration? Here are a few tips to get you started:

Make time for self-reflection: One can set aside time each day or week to reflect on their thoughts, feelings, and experiences, which can be as simple as reflecting, journaling, or meditating.

The process of reflection is examining one's thoughts, feelings, and behaviors. It is a way of exploring and understanding oneself and the world. Reflection can be a valuable tool for personal growth and development. It can help individuals learn more about themselves and identify areas they want to change.

When we reflect, we are essentially looking back at something - whether it be an experience, a situation, or a piece of information. We need to reflect to understand the meaning of what we have experienced and make sense of it. But unfortunately, when attempting to recall what happened, we often only remember the bare facts rather than the nuances or subtleties that can give us a deeper understanding.

Reflection allows us to explore our thoughts and feelings in a safe and non-judgmental space. It is a way of giving ourselves time and space to process our experiences and to make meaning of them. Through reflection, we can gain insights into ourselves and our behaviors and learn how to make better choices in the future.

If you struggle to make sense of something that has happened or are stuck in a difficult situation, taking time to reflect can be very helpful. Here are some tips for how to remember:

1. Identify your intention for reflection. What do you hope to gain from reflecting on this experience?
2. Find a comfortable and safe place to reflect. You could choose a quiet and private location, or you could opt to be accompanied by a trusted friend or therapist.
3. Write down your thoughts and feelings. You can write this in a journal or brainstorm on paper.
4. Allow yourself to explore your thoughts and feelings without judgment.
5. Once you have spent time reflecting, see if you can identify any patterns or themes in your thoughts and behaviors.
6. Ask yourself what you can learn from this experience and how you can apply this learning to your life.
7. Finally, be gentle with yourself. Reflection can be a complex process, but it can also be gratifying. Allow yourself the time and space to explore your thoughts and feelings and learn from them.

When considering starting a journal, you should keep a few things in mind. First, choose a journal that is comfortable for you to write in. This can be a physical journal you write in by hand or a digital journal you type into on your computer or phone.

Next, decide how often you want to journal. Some people journal daily, while others journal once a week or even once a month. There is no right or wrong answer here - it's all about what works for you.

Finally, set aside time to write in your journal daily or weekly. This can be first thing in the morning, before bed, or during your lunch break at work. If you can't find a block of time that works for you, try setting a timer for 10-15 minutes and writing until the timer goes off.

If you need help with what to write about, start by brainstorming a few topics. Some prompts you might want to consider:

- What were the highlights of your day?
- What are you grateful for?
- What are your hopes and fears for the future?
- What are your thoughts on a current event or news story?
- What are you struggling with right now?
- What positive things have happened in your life recently?

No matter what you choose to write about, remember there are no journaling rules. Most importantly, you are honest with yourself and allow your thoughts and feelings to flow freely.

Meditation is a mental and physical practice that has many benefits. It can help improve focus and concentration, reduce stress and anxiety, and promote relaxation. There are many different types of meditation, but all involve focusing on the breath and mindfully observing thoughts and feelings without judgment.

Meditation can promote relaxation, reduce stress, and increase focus and concentration. There are many different types of meditation, but they all involve sitting quietly and focusing on your breath.

Meditation has been an ancient practice for centuries to promote relaxation, peace of mind, and self-awareness. There are many different types of meditation, but the basic premise is to focus on a single object or thought and clear your mind of all other distractions. You can do this by focusing on your breath, a mantra, or a specific question or problem you are trying to solve. The goal is to achieve a state of mindfulness or complete focus and awareness.

Meditation is a mental and physical practice that has many benefits. It can help improve focus and concentration, reduce stress and anxiety, and promote relaxation. There are many different types of meditation, but all involve focusing on the breath and mindfully observing thoughts and feelings without judgment.

Meditation is an effective way to focus and calm the mind. It is a simple yet powerful tool that can reduce stress, promote relaxation, and improve focus and concentration. Meditating, you focus on your breath and allow all other thoughts and feelings to pass through your mind without judgment. Becoming more aware of your thoughts and feelings and letting go of any that no longer serve you can be achieved through this practice.

There are many different types of meditation, but all involve focusing on the breath and mindfully observing thoughts and feelings without judgment. Some common types of meditation include mindfulness meditation, loving-kindness meditation, and visualization meditation.

- **Mindfulness meditation** is a type of meditation that involves focusing on the present moment. For example, you focus on your breath and let all other thoughts and feelings pass through your mind without judgment. By practicing mindfulness, one can become more aware of their thoughts and feelings and let go of those no longer beneficial.

- **Loving-kindness meditation** is a type of meditation that involves sending thoughts of love and kindness to yourself and others. This meditation can help you develop compassion and understanding for yourself and others.
- **Visualization meditation** is a type of meditation that involves visualizing a positive outcome for yourself or a situation. This type of meditation can help you to achieve your goals and to create a more positive outlook on life.

Meditation is a simple yet powerful way to improve mental and physical health. It can help to reduce stress and anxiety, to promote relaxation, and to enhance focus and concentration. There are many different types of meditation, but all involve focusing on the breath and mindfully observing thoughts and feelings without judgment.

- **Seek feedback:** Asking others for feedback on strengths and weaknesses is a great way to gain an outside perspective and identify areas for improvement.
- **Take personality tests:** Many free online tests can help you gain insights into your personality traits, strengths, and weaknesses.
- **Practice self-compassion:** Remember that self-exploration is not about judging or criticizing yourself. Be kind and compassionate to yourself as you uncover new truths about yourself.

By gaining a deeper understanding of yourself, you'll be better equipped to navigate life's challenges, align your life with your values, and achieve your goals. So, take some time to explore who you are, and remember that the journey of self-exploration is lifelong.

Identifying Your Values

Identifying your values allows you to delve deeper into the guiding principles that shape your life and drive your decisions. Your values form the foundation of your identity, consisting of beliefs, ideals, and principles that matter most to you. Aligning with your values gives you a sense of purpose and fulfillment, while straying from them may leave you feeling lost or unfulfilled. Therefore, making your values a central focus of your life is crucial.

So, how can you identify your values? Here are a few steps to get you started:

- **Reflect on your experiences:** Think back on your life experiences - both positive and negative. What were the common themes or values that emerged? For example, did you consistently prioritize helping others, or did a need for adventure drive you?
- **Consider what you stand for:** What causes or issues matter most to you? What principles do you believe in, regardless of the situation?
- **Imagine your ideal world:** What values would be at the forefront if you could create the perfect world? Would it be one of love, justice, freedom, or something else entirely?
- **Prioritize your values:** Once you've identified your values, prioritize them. Which ones are the most important to you? Which ones do you want to focus on in your life right now?

It's important to note that your values may change over time. For example, what was important to you in the past may be less relevant now. Therefore, it's important to reassess your values and ensure they align with your current beliefs and priorities.

Living in alignment with your values requires courage and commitment. It means making choices that may not always be easy but align with your true self. When you align with your values, you'll feel a sense of purpose and fulfillment that can't be achieved by simply going through the motions.

So, my friends, take some time to reflect on your values. Identify the principles that matter most to you and make them a central focus of your life. When you live in alignment with your values, you'll create a life that's not only fulfilling but also impactful.

To further solidify your understanding of your values, consider the following exercises:

EXERCISE 1

Values Ranking Exercise: Make a list of your top 10 values and rank them in order of importance. Then, reflect on why you chose to prioritize each value in that order. This exercise will help you understand the hierarchy of your values and how they influence your decision-making.

To help you out here is a list of values that are commonly recognized:

1. Honesty
2. Integrity
3. Respect
4. Responsibility
5. Accountability
6. Empathy
7. Compassion
8. Kindness
9. Generosity
10. Fairness
11. Justice
12. Loyalty
13. Perseverance
14. Courage
15. Humility
16. Gratitude
17. Creativity
18. Innovation
19. Ambition
20. Diligence
21. Discipline
22. Authenticity
23. Trustworthiness
24. Patience
25. Wisdom

Note that this is not an exhaustive list, and different people may have different values that are important to them.

EXERCISE 2

Values Conflict Exercise: Identify a situation where you had to choose between two values that were in conflict with each other. For example, choosing between honesty and loyalty. Reflect on how you made the decision and what values ultimately guided your choice. This exercise will help you understand how your values interact with each other and the role they play in your decision-making.

EXERCISE 3

Values Alignment Exercise: Take a look at your current life and assess how aligned it is with your values. Are you living in alignment with your values, or are there areas where you're straying from them? If there are areas of misalignment, reflect on how you can adjust your life to bring it back into alignment with your values.

Remember, identifying your values is the first step in living a life of purpose and fulfillment. It's up to you to take action and make choices that align with your values. When you do, you'll create a life worth living.

Assessing Your Strengths and Weaknesses

Your strengths are the things that come naturally to you, the areas where you excel without much effort. Your weaknesses, on the other hand, are the areas where you struggle or need improvement. By identifying your strengths and weaknesses, you can build on your strengths and improve your weaknesses to become the best version of yourself.

Here are a few steps to assess your strengths and weaknesses:

- **Reflect on your past successes and failures:** Think back on your past experiences and identify the areas where you excelled and the areas where you struggled. What strengths did you rely on to achieve your successes? What weaknesses held you back from reaching your full potential?
- **Ask for feedback:** Obtain feedback from people in your personal and professional circles by requesting their input on identifying your strengths and areas that require improvement. Feedback can provide insight into blind spots and areas to focus on for personal growth.
- **Take a personality test:** Many personality tests can help you identify strengths and weaknesses. These tests can give you a more objective perspective on your personality and help you identify areas where you can improve.
- **Identify your passions:** What activities or hobbies do you enjoy the most? These are areas where you have natural strengths. By pursuing your desires, you can develop your strengths even further.

Once you've identified your strengths and weaknesses, developing a plan to build on your strengths and improve your weaknesses is important. Here are a few tips to get started:

- **Leverage your strengths:** Focus on activities and projects that allow you to use your strengths to their fullest potential. By doing so, you'll excel in those areas and gain confidence and satisfaction.
- **Seek support for your weaknesses:** Identify areas where improvement is needed and seek support from people

around. Options may include taking classes, seeking mentorship, or working with a coach.

- **Set goals:** Aligning your goals with your values and leveraging your strengths provide a clear direction and a sense of purpose and help maintain motivation.

Assessing your strengths and weaknesses requires honesty and vulnerability. It's important to embrace your strengths and weaknesses rather than trying to hide or ignore them. By doing so, you'll be able to grow and develop in a way that aligns with your values and brings you fulfillment.

Discovering Your Passions

Passions are the activities or hobbies that bring you joy and fulfillment. By discovering your passions and incorporating them into your life, you'll experience greater purpose and happiness.

Let's explore some steps to discover your passions:

- **Reflect on your past experiences:** Reflect on your life and identify the most activities or hobbies you enjoyed. For instance, you might remember that you always loved playing the guitar as a kid or that you felt most alive on the basketball court. What were you doing when you felt the most engaged and energized?
- **Try new things:** Feel free to step outside your comfort zone and experiment with new activities or hobbies. For example, you could try a new workout class, take a cooking course, or learn a new instrument. Trying new things can help you discover new passions you didn't even know existed.

- **Pay attention to your emotions:** Notice how you feel when doing certain activities. For example, do you feel excited and energized or bored and drained? Attention to your feelings can help you identify activities that align with your passions. For example, you feel most active hiking in nature. In that case, this might be a sign that you're passionate about outdoor activities.
- **Identify your values:** Values often tie to passions. By knowing your values, narrowing down the search for passions and finding activities aligning with values is possible. For instance, the community is one of your core values, and a passion for volunteering or organizing community events may arise.

Once you've discovered your passions, it's important to incorporate them into your life. Here are a few examples:

- **Make time for your passions:** Allocate time for your passions by scheduling specific time slots on your calendar. For instance, if writing is your passion, you can set aside an hour daily. Using this approach, you can prioritize your desires and ensure time for activities that bring joy.
- **Share your passions with others:** Sharing your passions with others can help you connect with like-minded individuals and build a sense of community. For example, joining a photography club or sharing photos on social media are new opportunities and experiences that can arise. Pursuing a passion like photography can open up avenues for such opportunities.
- **Use your passions to set goals:** Incorporating your passions into your plans can help you stay motivated and focused and give you a sense of purpose. For instance, if

you're passionate about running, you could set a goal to run a marathon, which will help you stay motivated to achieve your goal.

Remember, discovering your passions requires an open mind and a willingness to try new things. Feel free to experiment with different activities and hobbies until you find what brings you joy and fulfillment.

Overcoming Limiting Beliefs

To overcome limited beliefs, we must first learn what limited beliefs are. Limiting beliefs are the negative thoughts and beliefs that hold you back from achieving your goals and living your best life. These beliefs can come from past experiences, societal expectations, or self-talk. They limit your potential and prevent you from achieving your dreams.

Let's explore some steps to overcome limiting beliefs.

- **Identify your limiting beliefs:** The first step to overcoming them is identifying them. Ask yourself, what negative thoughts or beliefs do I have about myself or my abilities? Then, write them down and take a close look at them. For example, you might believe that you need to be more intelligent to start your own business or that you're too old to learn a new skill.
- **Challenge your limiting beliefs:** Once you've identified them, challenge them. Ask yourself, is this belief true? Do you have evidence to support it? Frequently, you will discover that your limiting beliefs are not grounded in reality but in fear and self-doubt. For example, if you

believe that you need to be more intelligent to start your own business, challenge that belief by looking at successful entrepreneurs who started with no experience or education.

- **Reframe your limiting beliefs:** Instead of focusing on what you can't do, reframe your limiting beliefs into empowering beliefs. For example, if you believe you're too old to learn a new skill, reframe that belief by telling yourself that you're experienced and have the wisdom to excel.

- **Take action:** Finally, take action to overcome your limiting beliefs. Trying new things or seeking out the help of a mentor or coach might be necessary to achieve this. For example, if you need more confidence in public speaking, take a public speaking course or join a Toastmasters club.

Remember, your limiting beliefs are not facts but stories you tell yourself. You can overcome your limiting beliefs by identifying, challenging, and reframing them and achieving your full potential.

Let's examine some examples of limiting beliefs and how to overcome them.

"I'm not good enough": This common limiting belief keeps many people from pursuing their goals. Challenge this belief by examining your accomplishments and reminding yourself of your strengths. Reframe this belief by telling yourself that you can learn and grow.

"I don't have enough time": This limiting belief can prevent you from pursuing your passions and achieving your goals. So first, challenge this belief by examining how you spend your time and identifying areas where you can make more time for the things that matter. Then, reframe this belief by telling yourself you have control over your time and can prioritize your goals.

"I'm too old/young": Age is just a number and should not limit your potential. First, challenge this belief by looking at successful individuals who have achieved great things at different ages. Then, reframe this belief by telling yourself that age is a mindset and that you can achieve anything at any age.

Remember, overcoming limiting beliefs requires a willingness to challenge your thoughts and beliefs. By doing so, you can break free from the constraints of your limiting beliefs and achieve your full potential.

We've covered a lot of ground, from understanding the importance of self-exploration to identifying our values, passions, and strengths. We've also discussed the obstacles of limiting beliefs and how to overcome them.

Remember, self-mastery is a lifelong journey that requires continuous growth and self-improvement. Achieving it cannot happen overnight; instead, it is a process that demands dedication and perseverance.

As you move forward on this path to self-mastery, I want to leave you with a few key takeaways:

Self-exploration is a critical step in achieving self-mastery. It requires introspection, honesty, and a willingness to challenge your thoughts and beliefs.

Your values, passions, and strengths are the foundation of your self-mastery journey. They guide your decisions and help you stay true to yourself.

Limiting beliefs is the biggest obstacle to self-mastery. By identifying, challenging, and reframing them, you can break free from their constraints and achieve your full potential.

Finally, self-mastery is a journey, not a destination. It requires continuous growth, self-improvement, and a commitment to lifelong learning.

Story of Self-Exploration

Here is a true personal story of a celebrity who learned self-exploration:

Demi Lovato was known as a child for her incredible vocal talent and on-screen charisma. She quickly rose to fame and found herself at the center of attention in the entertainment industry. But behind the scenes, Demi struggled with addiction, mental health issues, and self-doubt.

In 2010, Demi made headlines when she checked into rehab for the first time at the age of 18. She had been struggling with bulimia, self-harm, and addiction to drugs and alcohol. While in treatment, Demi was diagnosed with bipolar disorder, which affects mood and energy levels.

Demi's journey to self-exploration didn't end with her time in rehab. In the following years, she continued to speak openly about her struggles with mental health and addiction. In addition, she worked with therapists and coaches to develop coping mechanisms and strategies for managing her symptoms.

In 2018, Demi experienced a near-fatal overdose and was rushed to the hospital. This was a wake-up call for Demi, who realized she needed to change her life significantly. So, she took a step back from the spotlight and focused on her mental and physical health.

During this time, Demi embarked on a journey of self-exploration. She began to explore her spirituality, learning about meditation and mindfulness practices. She also discovered the power of fitness and started working with a personal trainer to improve her physical health.

Demi's journey of self-exploration led her to discover a deep sense of self-love and acceptance. She began to embrace her flaws and recognize her inherent worth as a human being. She also found purpose in sharing her story with others and advocating for mental health awareness.

Today, Demi is a powerful voice in the mental health community. She continues to be open and honest about her struggles, using her platform to raise awareness and promote self-care. Her journey of self-exploration serves as a powerful reminder that no matter how successful or talented we may be, we all have our struggles and can benefit from a deeper understanding of ourselves.

Self-Assessment Questions

- What are the three things that I'm most grateful for in my life?
- In what ways am I living my life in alignment with my true purpose?
- How can I better connect with my inner wisdom and intuition?
- Am I allowing my past experiences to limit my present and future potential?
- What actions can I take to move closer to my goals and dreams today?
- Am I taking responsibility for my thoughts, feelings, and actions, or am I blaming others for my circumstances?
- How can I practice self-love and self-care in my daily life?
- What limiting beliefs are holding me back, and how can I shift them to more empowering beliefs?
- Am I living my life based on what others expect, or am I following my path and purpose?
- How can I positively impact the world around me and contribute to the greater good?

Self-Exploration Action Steps

- **Set aside time for introspection:** Schedule a regular time to reflect on your thoughts, feelings, and beliefs. This can be through journaling, meditation, or simply taking a quiet walk in nature.
- **Explore your values:** Identify what is most important to you and what you stand for. Make a list of your top values and think about how you can align your actions with them.
- **Identify your passions:** Think about what brings you joy and fulfillment. What activities do you find yourself losing track of time while doing? Identify your passions and consider how to incorporate them into your life.
- **Assess your strengths and weaknesses:** Take an honest inventory of your strengths and weaknesses. Identify areas where you excel and areas where you could use some improvement.
- **Challenge your limiting beliefs:** Identify any beliefs holding you back and challenge them. Are they really true? Can you reframe them in a more positive light?

Positive Affirmation

As you delve into the depths of self-exploration, you awaken dormant potentials and uncover hidden strengths. You celebrate your inherent gifts and talents, recognizing that they are precious treasures that have the power to shape your path and positively impact the world around you.

2

SELF-DISCOVERY

"You are not a drop in the ocean.
You are the entire ocean in a drop."
—Rumi

Self-discovery is the process of understanding who you are at your core - your values, beliefs, strengths, and weaknesses. It is about developing a deeper self-awareness and understanding of what makes you unique. When you know yourself, you can make better decisions, set clearer goals, and live more purposefully.

The benefits of self-discovery are numerous. Understanding your values can align your actions with what truly matters to you, leading to greater fulfillment and happiness. Self-discovery can also boost your self-confidence and improve your relationships with others.

Starting the self-discovery process can seem daunting, but anyone can embark on this journey with the right tools and mindset. The following sections will explore journaling, meditation, and mindfulness practices to help you reflect on your thoughts and feelings. We will also discuss the importance of seeking feedback and exploring new experiences and perspectives.

At the heart of self-discovery is embracing your authentic self. We will explore overcoming the fear of judgment and societal expectations to truly live as your authentic self. And, with a clear understanding of your values and passions, you can create a personal mission statement and discover your life purpose.

So, let us begin the journey of self-discovery together. The road may be challenging sometimes, but with dedication and the right mindset, you can uncover your true self and achieve self-mastery.

What is Self-Discovery?

Self-discovery is the process of understanding who you are at your core - your values, beliefs, strengths, and weaknesses. It is the foundation for achieving self-mastery and living a more fulfilling life. Self-discovery can help you make better decisions, set clearer goals, and live more purposefully.

At its core, self-discovery is about developing a deeper self-awareness. Reflecting on your thoughts and feelings and understanding why you act and think as you do is essential. In addition, self-discovery involves exploring the various parts of yourself - your fears, desires, and motivations - to gain a holistic understanding of who you are.

One way to begin the self-discovery process is through journaling. By writing down your thoughts and feelings, you can reflect on them and gain a deeper understanding of your inner workings. Another technique is mindfulness, which involves paying attention to the present moment and observing your thoughts without judgment.

Seeking feedback from others can also be a powerful tool for self-discovery. When we receive feedback, we can gain insight into our blind spots and areas for growth. This feedback can come from friends, family, coworkers, or mentors.

Exploring new experiences and perspectives can also be a valuable tool for self-discovery. You can challenge your assumptions and beliefs by stepping outside your comfort zone and gaining new insights.

Ultimately, self-discovery is about understanding what makes you unique and embracing your authentic self. Accepting yourself for who you are can build a strong foundation for self-mastery and live a more fulfilling life.

Benefits of Self-Discovery

Self-discovery has numerous benefits that can positively impact every aspect of your life. One of the key benefits of self-discovery is gaining clarity of purpose. You can sense direction and purpose by identifying your passions, strengths, and values. For instance, if you realize you're passionate about helping people, you may choose a career in social work or volunteer at a non-profit organization.

Another benefit of self-discovery is improved self-awareness. Self-reflection and introspection can help you become more aware of your emotions, behaviors, and thought patterns and how they impact your life. For example, suppose you're prone to negative self-talk. In that case, self-discovery can help you recognize this pattern and take steps to reframe your thoughts more positively.

Self-discovery can also lead to better relationships. Understanding yourself deeper allows you to communicate your needs and desires more effectively in relationships. You can also identify patterns and behaviors that may prevent you from forming deep, meaningful connections. For instance, if you struggle with trust issues, self-discovery can help you recognize this pattern and work towards building more trusting relationships.

Additionally, self-discovery can enhance personal growth. It can help you identify areas where you need to grow and develop and give you the tools to do so. For example, if you struggle with time management, self-discovery can help you identify the root cause and develop strategies to manage your time more effectively.

Another benefit of self-discovery is greater resilience. Understanding yourself better equips you to handle challenges and setbacks more effectively. As a result, you're more likely to bounce back from adversity and use it as an opportunity for growth. For example, experience a setback at work. Self-discovery can help you identify your strengths and plan to overcome the obstacle.

Finally, self-discovery can lead to improved decision-making. Making decisions that align with your true self is easier when you're clear on your values, goals, and purpose. You're less likely to be swayed by external pressures or make choices that don't serve your best interests. For instance, if you're considering a job offer, self-discovery can help you assess whether the opportunity aligns with your values and goals.

How to Start the Self-Discovery Process

The self-discovery process can feel overwhelming, but achieving personal growth and fulfillment is necessary. Here are some practical steps to help you begin:

Firstly, it is crucial to set aside dedicated time for self-reflection. There are various ways to clear your mind, such as meditation, journaling, or walking. This time allows you to ponder your life, aspirations, and values and think critically about what truly matters to you.

Next, it is crucial to question your assumptions and beliefs. It is easy to become stuck in patterns of thinking that may be limiting your potential. Challenge yourself to reconsider these assumptions and see if they align with your values and aspirations. Doing so may open up new avenues for personal growth.

Taking personality assessments, such as the Myers-Briggs Type Indicator or the Enneagram, can provide valuable insights into your personality traits, strengths, and weaknesses. These assessments can help you better understand yourself and give a roadmap for personal growth.

In addition, trying new things is an excellent way to learn more about yourself. One way to broaden your horizons is by experimenting with different activities, such as picking up new hobbies, traveling to unfamiliar destinations, or embarking on novel adventures. You may uncover new interests and passions and gain a fresh perspective by stepping outside your comfort zone.

Finally, seeking feedback can provide valuable insight into how others perceive you and help you identify areas for personal growth. Feedback from trusted friends, family members, or colleagues can give a fresh perspective on your strengths and weaknesses.

For example, if you have always been interested in art but have never explored your creative side, consider taking an art class or attending a local exhibit. If you have always been interested in entrepreneurship but have never pursued it, try starting a small business on the side. These experiences can provide valuable insights into what truly drives you and give you a greater sense of purpose.

Starting the self-discovery process requires a willingness to be open to new experiences, question your assumptions, and seek feedback from others. By committing to this journey, you will better understand yourself and develop the tools to live a more fulfilling life.

Identifying Your Mission Statement

Identifying your mission statement is a crucial step in the self-discovery process. It is a declaration of who you are, what you stand for, and a guiding principle for your life. Your mission statement should be unique to you and reflect your values, strengths, passions, and goals.

To begin crafting your mission statement, start by asking yourself some fundamental questions. What are the things that matter most to you? What are your greatest strengths? What motivates you to get out of bed every day? What do you want to achieve in life? Then, take some time to reflect on these questions and write down your answers.

Next, consider the impact you want to have on the world around you. What do you want your legacy to be? What do you want to be remembered for? Finally, think about how you can use your strengths and passions to make a positive difference in the lives of others.

Your mission statement should be concise, clear, and powerful. It should be something you can easily remember and recite to yourself as a reminder of who you are and what you stand for. Here are some examples of personal mission statements:

- To inspire others to live their best lives through the power of positivity and personal growth.
- To use my creativity and passion for design to make the world a more beautiful and functional place.
- To empower people to overcome their limiting beliefs and achieve their full potential.
- To be a loving and supportive partner, parent, and friend, and to always show up for the people I care about.
- To use my skills and knowledge to help protect and preserve the environment for future generations.

Remember that your mission statement is not set in stone and can evolve as you grow and learn. The important thing is to take the time to reflect on who you are and what you want to achieve and to create a guiding principle that will help you stay focused on your goals and live a fulfilling life.

Embracing Your Authentic Self

Embracing your authentic self is an essential part of the self-discovery journey. It means accepting and expressing your true self without fear or shame, regardless of external pressures or opinions. It is a way of living aligned with your core values, beliefs, and personality traits. However, many struggle with this step due to societal expectations and fear of rejection or criticism.

One of the first steps towards embracing your authentic self is to become aware of your values, beliefs, and priorities. These are the guiding principles that shape your life and determine the decisions you make. Identifying and living by your values can help you build meaningful and fulfilling relationships and guide you toward a more purposeful career and lifestyle.

Another aspect of embracing your authentic self is to let go of self-judgment and perfectionism. Many people set high expectations for themselves, leading to a never-ending cycle of self-criticism and disappointment. It's important to remember that everyone makes mistakes and that they are essential for personal growth and learning. Instead of striving for perfection, focus on progress and learning from your mistakes.

Practicing self-compassion is also crucial when it comes to embracing your authentic self. Self-compassion means treating yourself with kindness and understanding, just as you would with a close friend. It involves acknowledging and accepting your imperfections and recognizing your strengths and achievements. When you practice self-compassion, you create a nurturing environment that promotes self-growth and confidence.

Lastly, embracing your authentic self is an ongoing process that requires consistent self-reflection and self-awareness. As you grow and change, so do your values, beliefs, and priorities. Therefore, it's essential to regularly check in with yourself and reflect on how you're living your life. Are your actions aligned with your values? Are you expressing your true self? What changes can you make to live a more authentic life?

Embracing your authentic self is a powerful tool for personal growth and self-discovery. By accepting and expressing your true self, you can lead a more fulfilling life and inspire others to do the same. However, it requires self-awareness, self-compassion, and a willingness to let go of external pressures and expectations.

Discovering Your Life Purpose

Discovering your life purpose can be a challenging but rewarding process. It involves looking honestly at yourself and exploring what drives and inspires you. By discovering your life purpose, you can gain a sense of direction, fulfillment, and motivation in all aspects of your life.

To discover your life purpose, reflect on your values, strengths, passions, and interests. For example, ask yourself questions like, "What do I love doing?" or "What am I most proud of in my life?" This can help you uncover what truly brings you joy and fulfillment.

Another helpful exercise is to imagine yourself at the end of your life, looking back on your experiences. What would you want to have accomplished? What would you want to be remembered for? This can help you identify what truly matters to you and what kind of impact you want.

It's important to note that discovering your life purpose is not a one-time event but a continual process of self-discovery and growth. Your life purpose may evolve and change over time, and that's okay. It's essential to remain open and flexible as you continue to explore and discover new things about yourself and your passions.

For example, someone discovers they are passionate about environmental sustainability. They may start by volunteering for local organizations or attending events to learn more about the topic. Over time, they may pursue a career in the field or even start their organization to make a larger impact.

Discovering your life purpose is about connecting with your true self and living a life that aligns with your values and passions. It's a journey that can be challenging, but the rewards of living a purpose-driven life are immeasurable.

Story of Self-Discovery

Dwayne "The Rock" Johnson is a celebrity who has openly spoken about his journey of self-discovery. Growing up, Dwayne faced many challenges, including financial and family issues. As a result, he struggled with depression, anxiety, and a lack of direction in his life.

Despite these challenges, Dwayne found solace in sports and fitness. He became a professional wrestler and then transitioned to a career in acting. However, even with his success, he still felt unfulfilled and lost.

It wasn't until he hit rock bottom that he realized he needed to focus on himself and his well-being. So, he stepped back from his busy schedule and prioritized self-care and self-discovery.

Through therapy, meditation, and journaling, Dwayne began to uncover his true values and priorities. He realized he wanted to use his platform to inspire and motivate others, which led him to start his own production company, Seven Bucks Productions.

Dwayne also started to open up about his struggles with mental health and the importance of seeking help. By sharing his own story, he has advocated for mental health awareness. He has inspired countless others to prioritize their well-being.

Through his journey of self-discovery, Dwayne has found a sense of purpose and fulfillment. He has learned to love and accept himself, flaws and all, and has used his experiences to help others do the same.

Dwayne's story is a reminder that self-discovery is an ongoing journey and that there is always time to start prioritizing your well-being. By focusing on yourself and your values, you can find a sense of purpose and fulfillment that allows you to show up as your best self in all areas of your life.

Self-Assessment Questions

- What is it that you truly desire and value in your life?
- Can you recall a time when you faced a challenge and successfully overcame it? How did you navigate through that experience?
- What are some of the positive qualities or strengths that others often recognize in you?
- Are there any recurring patterns or themes in your life that you have noticed? How do they influence your thoughts, emotions, and behaviors?
- How do you typically respond to change or uncertainty? Do you embrace it, resist it, or find a balance between the two?
- What are some of your most deeply held beliefs or convictions? How do they shape your perspective and actions?
- When do you feel most energized, inspired, or in alignment with your true self? What activities or environments contribute to this state?
- Are there any aspects of your life where you feel a sense of dissatisfaction or longing for something more? What might be underlying those feelings?
- How do you typically approach and navigate relationships with others? What patterns or dynamics tend to emerge?
- Reflect on a time when you felt truly connected to your inner self or experienced a profound sense of fulfillment. What were the circumstances or factors that contributed to that experience?

Self-Discovery Action Steps

- **Reflect on your values:** Take time to think about what is truly important to you. Write down a list of your top values and consider how to align with them.
- **Identify your strengths and weaknesses:** Take an honest look at your skills and abilities. Make a list of your strengths and weaknesses and think about how you can use your strengths to achieve your goals while also working on improving your weaknesses.
- **Explore your passions:** List the activities, hobbies, and interests that bring you joy and fulfillment. Make time for these things in your life and explore new passions.
- **Create a personal mission statement:** Write down a statement representing who you are and what you want to achieve. Use this statement as a guide for making decisions and taking action in your life.
- **Embrace your authentic self:** Let go of any fears or insecurities that may hold you back from being your true self. Embrace your uniqueness and allow yourself to shine.
- **Discover your life purpose:** Reflect on your passions, values, and strengths to determine your life purpose. Consider how you can use your talents and abilities to impact the world positively.

Positive Affirmation

With every breath you take, you move closer to your most authentic self. Embrace the process of self-discovery with an open heart and a curious mind. Know that within you lies a universe waiting to be explored, and as you delve deeper into your essence, you unveil the beauty that has always been there, patiently awaiting your discovery.

3

SELF-UNDERSTANDING

"To know yourself as the Being underneath the thinker,
the stillness underneath the mental noise, the love, and joy
underneath the pain, is freedom, salvation, enlightenment."
—*Eckhart Tolle*

As we start understanding ourselves, we gain a deeper awareness of what makes us tick. Is it our motivations, our strengths, and our weaknesses? It does not matter what it is. What matters is that you understand yourself. You are shining a light on the inner workings of your minds and souls, allowing yourself to see yourself more clearly to make informed decisions about your lives.

Let me give you an example. Imagine you're trying to improve your communication skills, but you find yourself constantly getting defensive in conversations. I know I have done that in the past. Without self-understanding, you might not recognize that this defensiveness stems from your fear of vulnerability. However, by taking the time to understand yourself better, you can identify this underlying fear and work on overcoming it. With this knowledge, you can develop more effective communication skills, leading to more fulfilling relationships and better personal growth.

In this chapter, we will explore the process of self-understanding, the tools and techniques you can use to gain a deeper understanding of yourself, and the common obstacles you may face. We will also examine the power of self-understanding in achieving self-mastery and fulfilling your potential.

By gaining a deeper awareness of ourselves, we can make informed decisions and take intentional actions toward achieving our goals. So, let's dive in and discover the power of self-understanding together!

What is Self-Understanding?

Self-understanding allows us to make better decisions and take intentional actions toward achieving our goals by understanding ourselves better, our thoughts, emotions, beliefs, and behaviors.

There was a time in my life I struggled with self-confidence, had negative self-talk, and allowed limited beliefs to hold me back. But through self-awareness and self-understanding, I recognized the negative self-talk. I began living more positively by listening to positive affirmations and creating positive social media posts. I began to recognize my strengths and started to focus on them, which increased my confidence and growth.

Furthermore, self-understanding enables us to set more meaningful personal goals. When we deeply understand our motivations, strengths, and weaknesses, we can set goals that align with our values and capitalize on our strengths. We can also identify areas needing improvement and develop new skills to achieve our objectives.

For example, someone wants to become a better public speaker. Through self-understanding, they may recognize that they struggle with public speaking due to a fear of judgment from others. With this awareness, they can develop their confidence and presentation skills to become more effective speakers. They can increase their self-esteem and achieve personal growth by setting and working towards this goal.

Lastly, self-understanding is the foundation of self-acceptance, an essential element of personal development. When we understand ourselves better, we can accept ourselves for who we are, including our strengths and weaknesses. In addition, self-acceptance allows us to develop self-love, vital to living a fulfilling life.

For instance, imagine someone who struggles with body image issues. Without self-understanding, they may feel ashamed or embarrassed about their appearance, leading to negative self-talk and low self-esteem. However, with self-understanding, they can recognize their body image issues and develop a more positive self-image. Through self-acceptance, they can learn to love themselves for who they are, regardless of their physical appearance.

Self-understanding is crucial for personal growth and self-mastery. By developing self-awareness, we can identify our strengths and weaknesses, set meaningful goals, and cultivate self-acceptance and self-love. So, let's commit to this journey of self-discovery and take the first step toward a more fulfilling life!

The Process of Self-Understanding

Let's explore how to comprehend oneself. Through self-reflection and introspection, one can begin the process of developing self-understanding. Asking ourselves probing questions about our motivations and ideals will help us better understand our thoughts, feelings, and behaviors. Self-reflection is crucial for personal development as it helps us better understand ourselves.

Let's take the case of someone who wishes to improve time management. Individuals may understand through introspection that their tendency to procrastinate stems from either a fear of failure or a lack of self-discipline. Therefore, they can create tactics to combat procrastination and work more productively towards their goals by being aware of these underlying reasons.

The next step towards self-understanding is to identify personal biases and blind spots. These hidden biases or beliefs influence our thoughts and actions without realizing them. Recognizing and challenging our preconceptions can help us better understand ourselves and make more informed decisions.

Consider someone who has trouble exercising self-control regarding food, for instance. Some individuals may need to realize that they rely on food for comfort, leading them to overeat or engage in binge eating habits. However, they can attain personal growth and a more balanced relationship with food by becoming aware of this bias and combating it with healthy coping techniques like exercise or journaling.

The process of self-understanding also calls for an open and curious mindset. Even when unpleasant or complicated, we must approach ourselves with curiosity and want to learn. By adopting this mindset, we can eliminate limiting beliefs and better understand ourselves and the world.

The process of self-understanding requires self-reflection, identifying personal biases and blind spots, and approaching ourselves with an open and curious mindset. By embracing this process, we can better understand ourselves, overcome our limitations, and achieve personal growth. So, let's commit to this journey of self-discovery and become the best versions of ourselves!

Tools and Techniques for Self-Understanding

Let's discuss some practical methods and tools for achieving self-understanding

Developing self-understanding can be accomplished through effective techniques such as meditation and mindfulness. By engaging in these practices, we can better comprehend ourselves by tuning into our thoughts, emotions, and bodily sensations. For example, practicing mindfulness through meditation can cultivate an objective awareness of our thoughts and feelings, allowing us to understand ourselves better.

For example, someone dealing with anxiety can utilize mindfulness to maintain clarity while observing their anxious thoughts. Through consistent mindfulness practice, they can enhance self-understanding and gain better control over their anxiety.

Likewise, individuals grappling with self-doubt can employ journaling to examine their anxieties and negative thoughts. By recording their ideas and feelings and reviewing them, they can gain fresh perspectives on their inner world, paving the way for self-improvement plans.

In addition to these techniques, seeking advice and encouragement from others is a crucial aspect of self-understanding. We all possess biases and blind spots that hinder our objective perception. We can obtain valuable insights into ourselves and our behaviors by soliciting constructive criticism from trusted friends, family members, or professionals.

For instance, a person struggling with effective communication can seek feedback from a communication coach or therapist to identify their strengths and limitations. Then, working with a professional, they can develop strategies for improvement and uncover new insights about their communication style.

Lastly, psychological and personality assessments can serve as valuable resources for self-understanding. These evaluations provide information about our personality traits, strengths, and weaknesses, enabling us to understand ourselves and our behaviors better.

For instance, an individual might take a personality test to gain insights into their leadership, decision-making, and communication styles. With this knowledge, they can develop personal growth strategies and make more informed decisions.

In conclusion, a range of practical methods and tools can aid us in pursuing self-understanding. Writing, meditation, seeking feedback, and reflection contribute to our self-awareness and personal development. Let us, therefore, commit to employing these methods to enhance our understanding of ourselves and further our personal growth.

Common Obstacles to Self-Understanding

One of the biggest obstacles to self-understanding is fear and resistance to change. We like being comfortable, and change can be challenging for some. Some see change as an opportunity for growth, and others perceive it as disruptive.

Nonetheless, we hesitate to confront our emotions, beliefs, or convictions. However, it is essential to recognize that change is necessary for personal growth and that facing our fears and discomfort is a crucial step toward self-understanding.

For example, someone struggling with a fear of public speaking may resist practicing their skills because it brings up feelings of anxiety and fear. However, by recognizing and working through the fear, they can develop greater self-understanding and achieve personal growth

Another obstacle to self-understanding is negative self-talk and limiting beliefs. These thoughts and beliefs can hold us back from achieving our full potential and often stem from past experiences or societal conditioning. However, we can better understand ourselves and our behavior by challenging these negative thoughts and beliefs.

For instance, someone struggling with low self-esteem may have internalized societal messages or past experiences that they are not good enough. They can develop greater self-understanding and confidence by challenging and replacing these beliefs with more positive and empowering ones.

Cultural and social conditioning can also be an obstacle to self-understanding. Our upbringing, cultural background, and societal norms can shape our beliefs, values, and behavior, often without us realizing it. However, we can better understand ourselves and our actions by becoming aware of these influences.

For example, someone from a culture that values collectivism may struggle with individualism and not realize how cultural conditioning impacts their behavior. By recognizing these influences, they can gain greater self-understanding and develop strategies for personal growth.

So, how can we overcome these obstacles to self-understanding? One strategy is to practice self-compassion and non-judgment. By accepting ourselves and our experiences without judgment, we can create a safe and supportive environment for personal growth.

Another strategy is to seek support from others, whether through therapy, coaching, or peer support groups. By connecting with others with similar experiences, we can gain new insights and perspectives on ourselves and our behavior.

There are many obstacles to self-understanding, but with courage, self-compassion, and support from others, we can overcome them and achieve personal growth. So, let's commit to challenging our fears and negative beliefs, recognizing our cultural conditioning, and seeking support to become our best versions.

The Power of Self-Understanding

Self-understanding is essential for achieving self-mastery as well as personal development. A comprehensive awareness of ourselves can help us communicate and interact with others more effectively, become more self-aware, and grow emotionally intelligent.

As our understanding of ourselves grows, so does our self-awareness. We can recognize our unique characteristics, weaknesses, and habits. Gaining a better understanding of ourselves allows us to identify areas for improvement and take steps toward becoming the best possible versions of ourselves. For instance, someone aware of their procrastinating tendencies can improve their time management abilities and boost their productivity.

Developing emotional intelligence requires self-awareness, recognizing and managing our emotions and those of others. Understanding ourselves better can create greater empathy and compassion toward others, leading to more positive and fulfilling relationships.

For example, someone who has worked through their insecurities and self-doubt may better understand and support a partner going through a similar experience.

Furthermore, self-understanding allows us to communicate more effectively with others. When we understand ourselves better, we can express our thoughts and feelings more clearly and authentically, leading to more meaningful and productive conversations. Additionally, we can better understand the perspectives and needs of others, which can help us to build stronger relationships.

Finally, achieving self-understanding is essential for fulfilling our potential and achieving personal growth. By gaining an understanding of ourselves and our motivations, we can establish goals that are in line with our values and aspirations. We can lead more fulfilling and purposeful lives by working towards these goals.

For instance, someone who has developed a deep understanding of their passions and interests may pursue a career that aligns with those values, leading to greater job satisfaction and fulfillment.

Self-understanding is a crucial step toward achieving self-mastery. It allows us to become more self-aware, develop greater emotional intelligence, improve our relationships and communication, and fulfill our potential. So, let's commit to understanding ourselves better. We should acknowledge our strengths and weaknesses and work towards becoming the best possible versions of ourselves.

Story of Self-Understanding

Oprah Winfrey, one of our time's most influential and successful media personalities, has often spoken about her journey to self-understanding. Yet, despite her success and fame, Oprah has been open about her struggles in her personal life, including a difficult childhood and battles with weight, abuse, and self-doubt.

In her early years, Oprah struggled with the trauma of sexual abuse and challenging family life. She turned to food for comfort, and by her early 20s, she had gained significant weight. It wasn't until she started working as a news anchor that she began to focus on her appearance and embarked on a weight loss journey.

However, despite her success in her career and weight loss, Oprah still struggled with feelings of inadequacy and a lack of self-understanding. As a result, she continued to use food as a coping mechanism, and her weight fluctuated throughout her career.

When Oprah started her talk show, The Oprah Winfrey Show, in the 1980s, she began to explore her inner world and work towards a deeper understanding of herself. Through her show, Oprah connected with experts in personal growth and self-help and began to share their teachings with her audience.

Oprah's journey to self-understanding involved a deep dive into her past, relationships, and beliefs about herself. She worked with therapists, spiritual teachers, and personal growth coaches to better understand who she was and what she wanted out of life.

Through this process, Oprah learned to let go of the need for external validation and trust her inner voice. She also learned to prioritize her well-being, setting boundaries and saying no to commitments that didn't align with her values and priorities.

Today, Oprah is a shining example of self-understanding and self-love. She has used her platform to inspire millions worldwide to embrace their inner journey and live their best lives. Oprah's story is a testament to the power of self-exploration and the incredible transformation possible when we are willing to look within and do the work to understand ourselves on a deeper level.

Self-Assessment Questions

- Have you ever taken a moment to reflect on your unique strengths and abilities, recognizing the infinite potential that lies within you?
- Can you recall a time when you faced a significant challenge or obstacle and managed to overcome it by tapping into your inner resources and resilience?
- How well do you understand your own values and beliefs, and how do they shape your decisions and actions in everyday life?
- Have you explored the depths of your emotions, allowing yourself to fully experience and comprehend the range of feelings that exist within you?
- Can you recognize and appreciate the power of your subconscious mind, understanding how it influences your thoughts, behaviors, and interactions with others?
- Are you aware of the unconscious patterns and habits that may be holding you back from reaching your full potential, and are you actively working towards transforming them?
- Have you cultivated a deep understanding of your own unique identity, recognizing the multitude of roles you play in different aspects of your life?
- How well do you comprehend the impact of your past experiences and childhood on your present thoughts, behaviors, and relationships?

- Are you attuned to your own needs and desires, actively seeking self-care and self-nurturing practices to enhance your overall well-being?
- Can you embrace and accept all aspects of yourself, including your vulnerabilities and imperfections, with a sense of compassion and self-acceptance?

Self-Understanding Action Steps

Here are some action steps to help you apply the concepts from the Self-Understanding chapter:

- **Journaling:** Daily reflection on your thoughts, feelings, and behaviors. Write down what you observe about yourself and any emerging patterns or insights.
- **Seek feedback:** Ask trusted friends or family members about your strengths, weaknesses, and blind spots. It's important to be receptive to constructive feedback and view it as a chance to develop and improve.
- **Take personality assessments:** To better understand your unique traits and tendencies.
- **Practice self-compassion:** As you discover new things about yourself, approach the process with self-compassion and an open mind. Accept your flaws and shortcomings and view them as chances to develop and better yourself.
- **Experiment with new experiences:** Try new things that push you outside your comfort zone. Doing this will give you a deeper insight into your general inclinations, preferences, and aversions.
- **Seek support:** If you find yourself struggling with difficult emotions or challenges during the self-understanding process, consider seeking the assistance of a therapist or

coach who can provide guidance and support throughout the process.

Remember, self-understanding is an ongoing journey that requires patience, curiosity, and a willingness to learn and grow. By taking consistent action steps and staying committed to the process, you can better understand yourself and cultivate greater self-awareness and personal growth.

Positive Affirmation

Embrace the dance of self-understanding, gracefully moving through the rhythm of introspection and reflection. Celebrate the complexities of your being, for within them lie the seeds of personal growth and transformation.

4

SELF-LOVE

*"Owning our story and loving ourselves through that process
is the bravest thing that we'll ever do."*
—*Brené Brown*

What is self-love? At the heart of self-love is accepting and caring for yourself just as you are. It means acknowledging your worth and treating yourself with the same compassion and kindness you would offer to someone you deeply care about.

Many of us have been taught to prioritize the needs of others before our own under the guise of being caring or humble. However, this mindset is counterproductive. It hinders our ability to impact those around us. We can only give our best when we first prioritize ourselves. Don't fall into the trap of self-sacrifice. Remember that taking care of yourself first gives you the energy, clarity, and strength to care for others in a way that makes a difference. So let go of the guilt and start prioritizing yourself - it's not selfish; it's essential for creating a better world for all.

Self-love is vital for your personal growth and happiness. When you love and respect yourself, you're more likely to make positive choices, set healthy boundaries, and confidently pursue your goals. You're also more equipped to handle life's challenges and setbacks, knowing you have a solid foundation of self-worth and inner strength.

In this chapter, we'll explore how you can cultivate self-love and develop a healthy, positive relationship with yourself. We'll discuss overcoming self-criticism, comparison, negative self-talk and learning to appreciate and celebrate all that makes you unique.

Through this chapter, you'll gain a deeper understanding of the importance of self-love and how it can positively impact every aspect of your life, from your relationships to your career and overall well-being. So, let's dive in and begin the journey toward a more fulfilling and joyful life fueled by the power of self-love.

Understanding Self-Love

Understanding self-love means recognizing and accepting your worthiness as a human being, prioritizing your well-being, and treating yourself with kindness, compassion, and respect. It involves cultivating a deep appreciation and acceptance for yourself, including all your strengths, weaknesses, and imperfections.

Self-love is recognizing that you deserve love and care just as much as anyone else. It's about acknowledging that you are a unique and valuable individual with talents, passions, and dreams. By embracing self-love, you can learn to celebrate your successes, forgive your mistakes, and treat yourself with the same compassion and understanding you would offer to a close friend or family member.

To truly understand self-love, it's essential to differentiate it from self-esteem. While self-esteem is often based on external factors such as accomplishments or the approval of others, self-love is an internal sense of appreciation and acceptance that is not dependent on outside validation. Self-love is about developing a deep and abiding relationship with yourself, regardless of external circumstances.

When you practice self-love, you can better show up fully in your relationships and the world around you. By caring for your physical, emotional, and spiritual needs, you can cultivate inner peace and fulfillment, allowing you to approach challenges with greater resilience and optimism. Additionally, by setting healthy boundaries and saying no to commitments that don't align with your values or priorities, you can create a greater sense of balance and harmony in your life. I know that saying no can be difficult because of a variety of reasons, like:

- **Social pressure:** Many of us feel the need to conform to societal norms and expectations or to meet the expectations of others to fit in or be accepted. It can be tough to say no to commitments that don't align with our values, such as attending social events that we don't enjoy or participating in activities that don't resonate with us.

- **Fear of missing out (FOMO):** It is a powerful motivator that can make it difficult to say no to commitments, even when we know they don't align with our values or priorities. For example, we may feel pressured to attend a party or event we're not interested in because we fear missing out on something important or exciting.

- **Guilt:** Saying no can trigger feelings of guilt or selfishness because society has conditioned many of us to prioritize the needs of others over our own. For example, we have already committed to too many things by declining a work assignment that doesn't align with our values or saying no to a friend who needs our help can make us feel guilty.

- **Career concerns:** In the workplace, saying no to commitments that don't align with our values or priorities can be difficult because of worries about career advancement or job security. For example, we may feel pressure to take on a project or task we don't believe in because we fear it will impact our chances of promotion or recognition.

- **Lack of self-awareness:** Sometimes, it can be hard to say yes to commitments that don't align with our values or priorities because we need to be fully aware of them.

We may have a vague sense that something needs to be corrected but need help articulating why or taking action to change it.

Ultimately, understanding self-love is an ongoing journey of self-discovery and growth. It is an independent practice that involves learning to listen to your needs and desires and honoring your unique path. By cultivating self-love, you can build a strong foundation for personal growth, happiness, and fulfillment and become the best version of yourself.

Benefits of Self-Love

One of the most significant benefits of self-love is improved mental and emotional health. When we love ourselves, we are more likely to practice self-care and engage in activities promoting well-being, such as exercise, meditation, and leisure time in nature. These practices help to reduce stress, anxiety, and depression, which can ultimately lead to a more positive and fulfilling life.

In addition to improved mental and emotional health, self-love can increase confidence and self-worth. When we truly love ourselves, we recognize our value and worthiness and are less likely to seek validation from others. As a result, greater self-assurance and a sense of inner peace can radiate outward.

Another benefit of self-love is better relationships with others. We can better love and accept others when we love and accept ourselves. As a result, we are more compassionate, empathetic, and understanding, which can lead to deeper connections and more fulfilling relationships.

Lastly, self-love can lead to more fulfilling life experiences. Confidence in ourselves and our abilities makes us more likely to take risks and pursue our dreams. New opportunities, adventures, and experiences can enrich our lives and bring us joy.

For example, a person who practices self-love may feel confident enough to pursue a new career or start a business, leading to financial abundance and personal fulfillment. Another person may have the courage to travel to a new country and experience a different culture, leading to personal growth and expanded perspectives.

The benefits of self-love are numerous and impactful. By prioritizing our well-being and practicing self-love, we can experience improved mental and emotional health, increased confidence and self-worth, better relationships, and more fulfilling life experiences.

Overcoming Obstacles to Self-Love

Overcoming obstacles to self-love can be a challenging journey, but it's one worth taking. Negative self-talk and limiting beliefs can prevent us from recognizing our true worth and potential. We may tell ourselves that we're not good enough, that we don't deserve happiness, or that we'll never achieve our goals. These thoughts can be incredibly damaging and hold us back from living our best lives.

Comparison and perfectionism are also common obstacles to self-love. For example, we may constantly compare ourselves to others, believing we could be more successful, attractive, and accomplished. Experiencing this can result in emotions of inferiority and uncertainty about oneself. Similarly, perfectionism can cause us to set impossibly high standards for ourselves, leading to a constant feeling of failure and disappointment.

Childhood traumas and conditioning can also significantly affect our ability to love ourselves. For example, suppose we grew up in an environment where We did not receive love or affection, consistently criticized or shamed. In that case, we might struggle to develop a positive self-image. It's essential to recognize that these experiences may have impacted us deeply, but they do not define us.

To overcome these obstacles, we must first become aware of them. We can start by focusing on our thoughts and identifying negative self-talk patterns. Once we recognize these patterns, we can challenge them by replacing them with positive affirmations and self-love practices.

We can also work on letting go of comparison and perfectionism by focusing on our journey and progress rather than constantly comparing ourselves to others. Practicing self-compassion and forgiveness can also help us overcome childhood traumas and conditioning, allowing us to develop more vital self-love and worth.

Remember, self-love is a journey; overcoming these obstacles takes time and effort. But with persistence and a commitment to self-growth, we can learn to love ourselves unconditionally and live a more fulfilling life.

Here are some additional details and examples for the topic of overcoming obstacles to self-love:

- **Negative self-talk and limiting beliefs:** Many of us have a critical inner voice that tells us we're not good enough, smart enough, or worthy of love and success. These negative self-beliefs can be deeply ingrained and hold us back from achieving our full potential. However, with practice, we can learn to recognize and challenge these thoughts, replacing them with more positive and empowering self-talk. For example, instead of saying, "I can't do this," try saying, "I can do this, and I am capable of figuring it out."

- **Comparison and perfectionism:** In today's society, it's easy to get caught up in comparing ourselves to others and striving for perfection. However, this can lead to feelings of inadequacy and self-doubt. Although to tackle difficulties, one must take action. Therefore, focusing on your progress and celebrating your successes is important instead of constantly comparing yourself to others. Additionally, embracing imperfection and recognizing that mistakes are growth opportunities can help shift your mindset towards self-love and self-acceptance.

- **Childhood traumas and conditioning:** Our childhood experiences and upbringing can significantly impact our self-image and ability to love ourselves. For instance, consider if you grew up in a household where you received constant criticism and felt like you could never meet the expectations set for you. In that case, you may struggle with self-esteem and self-love as an adult. Therefore, it's important to recognize the impact of these experiences and seek support to heal from past traumas and rewire negative thinking patterns. Therapy, self-help books, and support groups can all be helpful tools in this process.

Recognizing and overcoming these obstacles can cultivate greater self-love and live more fulfilling lives.

Another obstacle to self-love is the fear of vulnerability. A common belief is that showing vulnerability is a weakness and may result in judgment or rejection by others. This fear can prevent individuals from forming deep and meaningful connections with others and fully embracing their emotions and experiences. However, vulnerability is a strength, as it allows us to connect with others on a deeper level and fosters empathy and understanding. By recognizing the importance of vulnerability and taking small steps to practice it, individuals can overcome this obstacle and cultivate self-love.

Finally, another obstacle to self-love is the belief that it is selfish or self-indulgent. Some people feel guilty for prioritizing their needs and desires, believing they should always put others first. However, self-love is not about neglecting the needs of others or being selfish. Instead, it is about recognizing that taking care of ourselves is necessary to give to others and positively contribute to the world. When we love ourselves, we become better equipped to love and serve others, ultimately making a more meaningful impact.

It is important to practice self-awareness and self-compassion to overcome these obstacles to self-love. It's essential to acknowledge negative self-talk and limiting beliefs and take action to replace them with positive and empowering thoughts. It also consists in acknowledging and accepting our vulnerabilities and being kind and gentle with ourselves as we work through difficult emotions and experiences. By embracing self-love and practicing it consistently, we can experience its numerous benefits and live a happier, more fulfilled life.

Cultivating Self-Love

One way to cultivate self-love is to practice self-compassion. Self-compassion involves treating ourselves with kindness and understanding when we make mistakes or experience challenges. It means recognizing that we are human and that it is natural to struggle or fall short sometimes. By practicing self-compassion, we can avoid self-criticism and negative self-talk, which can erode our self-esteem and self-worth.

Another way to cultivate self-love is to set boundaries. When you set boundaries, you are saying no to commitments that don't align with your values or priorities and respecting your needs and limitations. It involves recognizing that we are responsible for our well-being and that saying no to others is sometimes necessary for our health and happiness. By setting boundaries, we can create space for the things that matter most to us and avoid overcommitting ourselves.

Engaging in activities that give us happiness and fulfillment, such as hobbies, creative pursuits, or spending time with loved ones, is crucial. Prioritizing what brings us joy can help us achieve inner peace and fulfillment, positively impacting all aspects of our lives.

Finally, cultivating self-love involves recognizing and challenging negative self-talk and limiting beliefs. Negative self-talk is the inner dialogue that can undermine our self-worth and confidence, while limiting beliefs are the beliefs that hold us back from achieving our goals and living our best lives. By recognizing and challenging these patterns, we can cultivate a more positive and empowering mindset that supports our growth and well-being.

Remember, cultivating self-love is a lifelong practice that requires patience, dedication, and commitment. But by prioritizing our well-being and treating ourselves with kindness and compassion, we can create a foundation for personal growth and happiness that extends into all areas of our lives. So, take the time to nurture your relationship with yourself, and watch as your inner peace and joy flourish.

Nurturing Self-Love in Relationships

Nurturing self-love in relationships is crucial to living a fulfilling life. It starts with setting boundaries and respecting yourself enough to communicate your needs and desires. Boundaries help you establish your limits and maintain your emotional and physical well-being, essential for a healthy relationship. For instance, you may set boundaries around how much time you spend with your partner or the type of communication that feels comfortable for you.

Setting healthy boundaries is essential to nurturing self-love, and it involves knowing your limits and communicating them to others. To set healthy boundaries, you must understand your values and needs so you know what is acceptable and unacceptable to you.

For example, you can start by identifying what behavior or situation makes you feel uncomfortable or drained and then communicating your limits to others. When setting boundaries, it's essential to be assertive but not aggressive or passive and to remember that your needs are just as valid as anyone else's. Examples of healthy boundaries include saying "no" when you feel overwhelmed or saying "stop" when someone disrespects you. By setting healthy boundaries, you show yourself and others that you respect yourself and create space for positive and loving relationships.

Healthy communication is another vital aspect of nurturing self-love in relationships. Effective communication lets you express your thoughts and feelings without fear of judgment or rejection. It also involves active listening, empathy, and understanding your partner's perspective. For example, you can cultivate healthy communication by practicing "I" instead of "you" statements. Instead of saying, "You never listen to me," you can say, "I feel unheard when I speak, and it makes me feel unimportant."

Another way to nurture self-love in relationships is by choosing supportive and loving relationships. Surrounding yourself with people who lift you and inspire you to be the best version of yourself can significantly impact your self-love journey. Seek relationships with people with similar values, beliefs, and goals. These relationships will help you grow and thrive, providing a safe space to be yourself and feel loved unconditionally.

Nurturing self-love in relationships involves setting boundaries, practicing healthy communication, and choosing supportive and loving relationships. By cultivating these practices, you can create a strong foundation for yourself, allowing you to approach relationships with confidence, authenticity, and self-love.

Story of Learning Self-love

Growing up, Mary always felt like she wasn't good enough. She constantly compared herself to others, feeling she didn't measure up. This feeling followed her into adulthood, and she struggled with anxiety and depression.

It wasn't until Mary hit rock bottom that she realized she needed to change. She had been in a toxic relationship that left her feeling drained and unfulfilled. She was constantly giving to her partner, neglecting her own needs and desires in the process.

One day, after another argument with her partner, Mary sat alone in her car, tears streaming down her face. At that moment, she realized that she needed to love and care for herself as much as she loved and cared for others.

Mary started by setting boundaries with her partner and prioritizing her own needs. She started exercising regularly, eating healthier, and doing activities that brought her joy. She also began practicing self-compassion, recognizing that it was okay to make mistakes and that she deserved love and acceptance just as she was.

As Mary continued to practice self-love, she noticed a shift in her life. Her relationships with others improved; she could show up as her best self and give from a place of abundance rather than depletion. She also found that her anxiety and depression lessened as she learned to accept herself as she was and recognize her inherent worthiness as a human being.

Today, Mary is thriving. She has a fulfilling career, a supportive group of friends, and a loving relationship with herself. However, she knows that cultivating self-love is an ongoing process. Still, she's committed to prioritizing her well-being and treating herself with the kindness, compassion, and respect she deserves.

Self-Assessment Questions

- What are the things that I appreciate about myself, both physically and mentally?
- How do I prioritize self-care in my daily routine?
- Am I kind to myself in how I speak and think about myself?
- Do I set boundaries to protect my emotional and mental well-being?
- What are my strengths, and how do I celebrate them?
- How do I practice forgiveness towards myself and others?
- How do I handle my mistakes and failures, and what do I learn from them?
- What activities bring me joy, and how often do I make time for them?
- Do I surround myself with people who lift me and support me?
- How do I practice self-compassion when I am going through a difficult time?

Self-Love Action Steps

Here are some action steps you can take to cultivate self-love:

- **Practice self-care:** Make time for activities that nourish your mind, body, and soul, such as exercise, meditation, and hobbies you enjoy.
- **Focus on your strengths:** Acknowledge and celebrate your strengths and accomplishments rather than dwelling on your weaknesses.
- **Practice self-compassion:** Be kind to yourself and forgive yourself for mistakes or shortcomings. Treat yourself with

the same compassion and understanding you would offer to a close friend.

- **Surround yourself with positivity:** Surround yourself with people who uplift and support you and minimize your exposure to negativity and toxic influences.
- **Set boundaries:** Establish clear boundaries with others to protect your time, energy, and well-being. Saying no to things that don't serve you is an act of self-love.
- **Challenge negative self-talk:** Notice and challenge negative self-talk, replacing it with positive affirmations and self-talk that reinforces self-love and self-acceptance.
- **Practice gratitude:** Cultivate a sense of gratitude for all the good things in your life and focus on what you have rather than what you lack.
- **Seek help if needed:** Don't be afraid to seek professional help if you struggle with self-love or other emotional issues. There is no shame in asking for help; it can be a powerful act of self-care and self-love.

Remember, self-love is a journey, not a destination. Cultivating takes time, effort, and patience, but the rewards are immeasurable. By taking these action steps, you can nourish your relationship with yourself and develop a greater sense of self-love and self-acceptance.

Positive Affirmation

Embrace the transformative power of self-love, dear soul, for it is the foundation upon which your most authentic and fulfilling life is built. As you love yourself unconditionally, you create a ripple effect of love that expands far beyond your own existence, touching the hearts of all whom you encounter.

5

SELF-TRANSFORMATION

"Transformation is not a future event; it is a present activity.
We must be willing to let go of the life we planned
so as to have the life that is waiting for us."
—*Joseph Campbell*

Regarding self-transformation, there is no timetable for when your transformation will occur. However, just as the caterpillar spins a cocoon around itself and undergoes a profound metamorphosis, emerging as a beautiful butterfly, we, too, have the power to transform ourselves into something new and extraordinary.

Like the caterpillar, we may sometimes feel stuck in our current form, limited by our beliefs or circumstances. But just as the caterpillar sheds its old skin and embraces a new form, we, too, can shed our old ways of thinking and embrace a new perspective.

And like the butterfly, we can spread our wings and soar, embracing new opportunities and experiences that we never thought possible. Through self-reflection, perseverance, and a willingness to grow and change, we can transform ourselves into something truly magnificent, just like the butterfly emerging from its cocoon.

What is Self-Transformation

Self-transformation is the art of molding oneself into a superior version of one's former self. It is a process of deep introspection and self-reflection, fueled by a burning desire to improve and excel in every area of life.

Self-transformation requires a fearless commitment to change and a willingness to confront one's flaws and weaknesses head-on. In addition, it demands a strategic approach, whereby one systematically identifies areas of weakness, develops a plan of action, and steps towards improvement.

The process of self-transformation is not for the faint of heart. It requires a strong will, unwavering determination, and an unrelenting pursuit of excellence. But the rewards are immeasurable for those willing to put in the work.

Self-transformation is a journey of self-discovery and personal growth, an opportunity to unlock one's true potential and become the best version of oneself. And for those who are willing to embark on this journey, the possibilities are limitless.

Importance of Self-Transformation

You see, personal growth is not a passive process. It requires a conscious decision to confront our limitations, shortcomings, and ingrained behavior patterns. By embarking on the path of self-transformation, we take control of our destiny and actively shape our lives according to our aspirations.

Self-transformation is a means of transcending mediocrity and rising above the masses. It allows us to shed the shackles of complacency and embrace a mindset of constant improvement. By continuously honing our skills, expanding our knowledge, and cultivating our strengths, we position ourselves as agents of change in a world that often settles for mediocrity.

But let me be clear; personal growth is not solely about accumulating knowledge or acquiring new skills. It goes much deeper than that. True self-transformation necessitates a fundamental shift in our core beliefs and values. It compels us to question our assumptions, challenge societal norms, and redefine the boundaries of what we deem possible.

The benefits of self-transformation extend far beyond the realm of personal growth alone. Success, in its various forms, be it financial, professional, or even interpersonal, is the natural byproduct of an individual who has undergone a profound transformation. As we develop the discipline, resilience, and strategic thinking that self-transformation entails, we become formidable forces capable of overcoming any obstacle.

Moreover, self-transformation instills within us a sense of purpose and authenticity. It allows us to align our actions with our true passions and desires, unleashing a reservoir of untapped potential. By tapping into our unique strengths and talents, we differentiate ourselves from the masses, carving out a niche that resonates with our true selves.

In essence, dear reader, self-transformation is the gateway to a life lived to its fullest potential. It catalyzes personal growth and is the key to achieving lasting success. So, embrace the transformative journey, for it is only through self-transformation that you will uncover the greatness that lies dormant within you.

Identifying the Need for Self-Transformation

As we go through life, it's easy to get caught up in our routines and habits, and we need to realize the areas in which we could improve to achieve our full potential.

Identifying the need for self-transformation requires an in-depth and honest assessment of our strengths and weaknesses. This can be challenging as it often requires us to confront our fears and vulnerabilities. However, it's essential to understand that self-transformation is a lifelong journey that can lead to personal growth and success.

One of the first steps towards self-transformation is identifying areas of your life that need improvement. These areas can vary from person to person. They can be related to various aspects of life, such as health, relationships, finances, and personal development. For example, you may recognize your unhealthy eating habits or struggle with managing your finances. By acknowledging these areas, you can take steps towards transformation and self-improvement.

It's also crucial to understand the consequences of not transforming. For example, we continue to ignore the areas where we need improvement. In that case, we may find ourselves stuck in patterns of behavior that hinder our growth and success. For example, if we struggle with self-discipline and fail to address it, we may only reach our full potential and achieve our goals.

However, the good news is that many individuals have transformed themselves and overcome their limitations. These individuals have demonstrated that we can change ourselves with dedication and commitment. Take the example of Jim Carrey, who grew up in poverty and faced numerous obstacles on his journey toward becoming a successful comedian and actor. Yet, through his perseverance and dedication, he transformed himself into one of the most celebrated comedians of our time.

Another example is Dwayne "The Rock" Johnson, who overcame multiple failures and setbacks before becoming a successful actor, producer, and entrepreneur. Through hard work and determination, he became one of the world's most recognizable and influential celebrities.

Identifying the need for self-transformation is crucial to achieving personal growth and success. By acknowledging the areas of our lives that require improvement and understanding the consequences of not transforming, we can begin our journey toward becoming the best version of ourselves. Let's take inspiration from the examples of those who have transformed themselves and committed to our transformation journey.

Developing a Growth Mindset

One of the keys to achieving self-transformation is cultivating a growth mindset. This means shifting from a fixed mindset - where we believe our abilities and intelligence are fixed and cannot be changed - to a growth mindset, where we understand that we can develop and improve our abilities through hard work and perseverance.

Understanding the difference between a fixed and a growth mindset is essential. Individuals with a fixed mindset tend to believe that their abilities and intelligence are set in stone and cannot be changed. As a result, they may shy away from challenges and view failure as a reflection of their abilities rather than an opportunity for growth. On the other hand, individuals with a growth mindset see challenges and setbacks as opportunities for learning and growth. They believe they can improve their skills and achieve their goals with effort and persistence.

Cultivating a growth mindset is crucial for fostering self-transformation. By embracing the belief that we can grow and improve, we open ourselves to new opportunities and challenges. As a result, we become more resilient in the face of setbacks and are more likely to persist in facing challenges.

Many successful individuals have developed a growth mindset and transformed themselves through hard work and perseverance. Take the example of Michael Jordan, who was cut from his high school basketball team but used this setback as motivation to work harder and become one of the greatest basketball players ever. Or consider the story of Thomas Edison, who failed over 1,000 times before inventing the light bulb. He famously said, "I have not failed. I've just found 10,000 ways that won't work."

Overall, cultivating a growth mindset is a powerful tool for self-transformation. By embracing the belief that we can improve and develop our abilities, we open ourselves to new possibilities and opportunities. So, let's begin cultivating our growth mindset and embrace the power of self-transformation.

The Power of Habits

Habits are crucial in shaping our thoughts, behaviors, and lives. Understanding how to identify and replace negative patterns with positive ones and developing new habits can be a powerful tool for self-transformation.

First, let's talk about the role of habits in self-transformation. Habits are ingrained patterns of behavior that are formed through repetition and practice. They can be positive and negative and significantly impact our ability to transform ourselves. By recognizing and changing our negative habits, we can create new neural pathways in our brains and establish positive practices that support our transformation.

Identifying and replacing negative habits with positive ones is key to self-transformation. Negative patterns can hold us back from achieving our full potential and be a significant barrier to personal growth. For example, we have a habit of procrastinating. In that case, it can prevent us from accomplishing our goals and reaching our full potential. By recognizing this negative habit and replacing it with a positive one, such as breaking tasks into smaller, more manageable chunks, we can transform ourselves and achieve our goals.

Developing new habits to support your transformation is another important step. By cultivating positive habits, we can create the momentum we need to achieve our goals and create lasting change. For example, we want to improve our physical health. In that case, we can develop a habit of exercising every day, or if we're going to improve our mental health, we can practice daily meditation.

Examples of individuals who have transformed themselves through habit change are abundant. Take the example of Tony Robbins, who transformed his life by developing new habits such as daily gratitude practice and exercise. He has also helped countless others, including CEOs, athletes, and everyday people, transform their lives through habit change.

Another example is Charles Duhigg, author of the book "The Power of Habit," who transformed his life by recognizing and changing his negative habits. Through this process, he was able to lose weight, improve his relationships, and achieve greater success in his career.

Habits play a powerful role in self-transformation. By understanding the role of habits in shaping our lives, identifying and replacing negative patterns with positive ones, and developing new habits to support our transformation, we can create lasting change and achieve our full potential. So, let's act today and cultivate positive habits supporting our journey toward self-transformation.

Overcoming Obstacles to Self-Transformation

Welcome to the section on overcoming obstacles to self-transformation. While self-transformation can be a powerful tool for personal growth and success, it can be challenging. In this section, we'll explore some common obstacles to self-transformation and strategies for overcoming them.

The first obstacle to self-transformation is limiting beliefs and fears. These beliefs and fears keep us from pursuing our goals and reaching our full potential. For example, you may believe you cannot achieve a specific goal or fear failure that stops you from taking risks. Therefore, it's essential to identify and address these obstacles head-on to overcome them. This may involve challenging your beliefs and reframing them in a more positive light or facing your fears and taking action despite them.

Dealing with setbacks and challenges is another common obstacle to self-transformation. We will inevitably face setbacks and challenges along the way, but how we deal with them. Rather than giving up when faced with obstacles, seeing them as opportunities for growth and learning is essential. This may involve adjusting your approach, seeking support from others, or simply persisting through the challenge.

The self-transformation process cannot overstate the importance of persistence and resilience. It's easy to become discouraged or give up when faced with obstacles, but it's essential to keep pushing forward. By staying committed to your goals and remaining resilient in the face of challenges, you'll build the strength and resilience needed to achieve true transformation.

Examples of individuals who overcame obstacles to transform themselves abound. One such example is J.K. Rowling, who faced numerous rejections before finally finding success as an author. Another example is Michael Jordan, who was cut from his high school basketball team before becoming one of the greatest basketball players ever. These individuals persisted through setbacks and challenges and ultimately achieved their goals through hard work and dedication.

Overcoming obstacles to self-transformation is essential to personal growth and success. By addressing limiting beliefs and fears, dealing with setbacks and challenges, and cultivating persistence and resilience, you can achieve true transformation and become the best version of yourself. So, let's commit to facing our obstacles head-on and moving forward with determination and purpose.

Embracing Change and Progress

As we venture on our path of self-mastery, we must remember that transformation is an essential and innate aspect of the journey. Just as a tree undergoes myriad cycles of expansion and contraction, so too shall you experience phases of development and strain. Therefore, it is crucial to prioritize your well-being by concentrating on your breath and vitality, enabling you to begin each day with vigor and resolve. By embracing change and advancement, we can sustain our motivation and advance closer to our desired destination.

One of the first steps towards embracing change is understanding the stages of change and how to navigate them. Change can be difficult and uncomfortable, and it's common to experience resistance and ambivalence. However, we can anticipate and overcome these obstacles by understanding the stages of change. The stages of change include pre-contemplation, contemplation, preparation, action, and maintenance. Each step requires different strategies and support, and it's essential to recognize where you are in the process and what you need to move forward.

Another important aspect of embracing change is recognizing progress and celebrating small wins. Transformation is a process that takes time and effort, and it's easy to become discouraged or lose sight of the progress we've made. However, we can stay motivated and build momentum toward our goals by celebrating small wins and recognizing our achievements.

Self-compassion is also crucial in the transformation process. Change can be difficult, and it's common to experience setbacks and challenges along the way. However, by practicing self-compassion and treating ourselves with kindness and understanding, we can overcome obstacles and continue moving forward.

There are numerous examples of people who have undergone a transformation and embraced change. Take the example of Michael

Jordan, who faced rejection and failure early in his basketball career. Yet, he became one of the greatest basketball players ever through persistence and dedication. Another example is Malala Yousafzai, who overcame cultural barriers and risked her life to fight for education and women's rights. As a result, she has become a global icon and advocate for change through courage and determination.

Embracing change and progress is a crucial part of the self-transformation process. By understanding the stages of change, recognizing progress, practicing self-compassion, and taking inspiration from others who have transformed, we can stay motivated and continue moving toward our goals. So, let's embrace change and progress and create the life we've always dreamed of.

Story of Self-Transformation

Inky Johnson's story of self-transformation is a truly inspiring one. Born and raised in one of the most dangerous neighborhoods in Atlanta, Georgia, Johnson grew up with few material possessions. But he had a strong family and a deep faith, which helped him overcome his many challenges.

Despite the obstacles he faced, Johnson was an incredibly talented football player. He received a scholarship to play football at the University of Tennessee. He was well on his way to achieving his dream of playing in the NFL.

However, Johnson's life was forever changed during a game against Air Force in 2006. A routine tackle left him with nerve damage in his right arm, effectively ending his football career and leaving him with a permanent disability.

At first, Johnson was devastated. He had dedicated his entire life to football and had never imagined a future without it. But he refused to let his injury define him. Instead, he turned to his faith, family, and love of learning to help him navigate this challenging time.

Johnson began reading books on personal development and attending seminars on leadership and motivation. He used these tools to cultivate a positive mindset and stay focused on his goals. He also underwent multiple surgeries and months of physical therapy to regain some use of his right arm.

Through hard work and perseverance, Johnson graduated from college with a degree in psychology, despite his injury. He then turned to motivational speaking, using his own story of triumph over adversity to inspire others to do the same.

Today, Inky Johnson is a renowned motivational speaker, author, and philanthropist known for his powerful message of hope and inspiration. He has spoken at countless schools, businesses, and conferences, sharing his story of resilience and perseverance and encouraging others to never give up on their dreams.

Johnson's message is powerful: no matter our challenges, we can overcome them and create the life we desire. His story is a reminder that transformation is possible, even in the face of seemingly insurmountable obstacles. And his example of dedication, hard work, and a positive mindset inspires us all.

Self-Assessment Questions

- In what ways have I adapted and transformed in response to life's challenges and obstacles?
- How have I utilized my unique resources and strengths to navigate through difficult situations and emerge stronger?
- What unconscious patterns or beliefs have hindered my personal growth, and how can I begin to reframe them to empower myself?
- How have I harnessed the power of my imagination and creativity to envision a future filled with growth and fulfillment?

- What subtle cues and signals have I noticed in my environment that can guide me toward transformative opportunities?
- How can I leverage my own personal experiences and learnings to inspire and motivate others on their own paths of transformation?
- In what ways can I embrace and celebrate the diversity of perspectives and approaches to self-transformation, opening myself up to new possibilities?
- What steps can I take to foster a deeper connection with my own unconscious mind, tapping into its vast wisdom and resources for personal transformation?
- How can I cultivate a mindset of curiosity and exploration, continuously seeking new knowledge and experiences to fuel my personal evolution?
- What small, incremental changes can I make in my daily routine that will contribute to my overall growth and transformation over time?

Self-Transformation Action Steps

Congratulations on taking the first step towards transforming yourself and creating your desired life. Throughout this chapter, we have explored the power of self-transformation and the actionable steps you can take to achieve your goals.

Start by identifying the areas of your life that you wish to transform and be clear about your goals and desired outcomes.

Use the power of your imagination to visualize yourself as having already achieved your desired state of being. Then, use your senses to create a vivid mental image of your ideal self.

Cultivate a sense of curiosity and openness to new experiences. Embrace the unknown and allow yourself to explore new paths and ideas.

Tap into your inner resources and strengths and use them to your advantage. For example, believe in yourself and your abilities, and use positive self-talk to bolster your confidence.

Be patient and persistent in your efforts. Remember that transformation is a process that takes time and effort to achieve lasting change.

Celebrate your successes along the way, no matter how small they may be. Use your progress as motivation to continue striving for even greater transformation.

Finally, continue to learn and grow, both intellectually and emotionally. Remain open to new ideas and perspectives and be willing to adapt and evolve as needed to achieve your goals.

Remember, my friend, that true transformation begins from within. Use these steps to tap into your inner resources and achieve your desired personal growth and transformation.

Setting specific, measurable, and achievable goals is important to start your self-transformation journey. Then, break down your larger goals into smaller, more manageable steps you can take action on today. Whether it's developing a growth mindset, replacing negative habits with positive ones, or overcoming limiting beliefs and fears, there are concrete actions you can take to transform yourself.

You should seek out the support and guidance of others as you pursue your transformation goals. Surround yourself with positive, supportive, and uplifting individuals, and seek the counsel and expertise of experts in your chosen field.

Consider finding an accountability partner who can help keep you on track and motivated. For example, you could seek the guidance and support of a friend, family member, coach, or mentor. Having someone to answer to and share your progress with will make you more likely to stay committed to your goals.

In addition, join a community of like-minded individuals who share your interests and passions. Community involvement can offer support, encouragement, and knowledge exchange.

Remember to celebrate your progress along the way, no matter how small it may seem. Staying motivated and focused on the positive changes you make will be easier with these helpful tips.

Finally, stay committed to your transformation goals and open to new ideas and perspectives. You can achieve the personal growth and transformation you desire with persistence and determination.

Ultimately, the journey of self-transformation is a lifelong process that requires dedication and persistence. Embrace the challenges and setbacks as opportunities for growth and continue to take action towards creating the life you desire. You have the power within you to transform yourself and achieve your wildest dreams. So, take action today and start your transformation journey. The world is waiting for you to shine.

Positive Affirmation

Like a phoenix rising from the ashes, you emerge from moments of adversity with renewed strength and purpose. Your spirit is unbreakable, and with every challenge, you uncover dormant reservoirs of resilience that propel you towards your highest potential.

6

SELF-MASTERY

"Mastering others is strength.
Mastering yourself is true power."
—*Lao Tzu*

Well done on reaching this milestone in your journey toward self-mastery! Your courage, commitment, and perseverance have brought you this far, and you should be proud of yourself. So, keep up the excellent work and keep pushing yourself to become the best version of yourself. Remember, the road to self-mastery is a challenging one. Still, the rewards are immeasurable for those willing to put in the effort. Self-mastery is a continuous journey of growth, evolution, and transformation. It requires an ongoing commitment to achieve your goals.

Your journey started with learning the basic foundation of self-mastery; self-exploration, where you took the time to delve deep into your thoughts, emotions, and behaviors. This foundation was the building block for self-discovery. You identify your values, strengths, and weaknesses through this process and understand what drives you.

The next step in your journey was self-understanding, as you gain deeper insights into your inner workings and how they relate to the world around you. Developing a keen awareness of your thoughts, feelings, and actions, and taking responsibility for them, was part of the process.

As you started learning more about yourself in the Self-love foundation, you accepted yourself for who you are. You treated yourself with kindness, compassion, and respect. When you love yourself, you are more likely to make decisions that align with your values and goals and less likely to be held back by self-doubt or insecurity.

Finally, in the self-transformation foundation, you actively worked to change aspects of yourself that are holding you back from reaching your full potential. Developing new habits, learning new skills, and adopting new behaviors were all involved in the process.

Remember, self-mastery is a journey, not a destination. It takes time, effort, and commitment, but the rewards are immeasurable. You can become the best version of yourself, overcome your fears and limitations, and achieve greatness. So, let's embark on this journey together and unleash our full potential!

I am thrilled to introduce you to the pinnacle of your journey so far - self-mastery. The power and importance of mastering oneself cannot be overstated, as it has the potential to bring about profound transformations in your life. In the following chapter, we will delve deep into the true meaning of self-mastery, its significance in achieving personal and professional goals, and most importantly, how you can begin your journey towards mastering yourself today. Let's embark on this exciting journey together!

Let's start by defining self-mastery; self-mastery refers to the ability to take charge of your thoughts, emotions, and actions to achieve your desired outcomes. It involves a constant pursuit of self-improvement and striving towards becoming the best version of yourself.

We must emphasize the importance of self-mastery in achieving personal and professional goals. It is the gateway to unleashing your full potential. When you control your thoughts, emotions, and actions, you are better equipped to make sound decisions, remain focused on your objectives, and surmount obstacles. With self-mastery, you can create a clear vision of what you aspire to achieve and possess the resilience and perseverance to bring it to fruition.

Let us take the example of an aspiring entrepreneur. Without self-mastery, it is easy to be sidetracked by distractions and fall prey to procrastination, making it challenging to stay on course. However, with self-mastery, one can overcome self-doubt, remain motivated, and take consistent action toward their goals.

Self-mastery comprises twelve vital elements: self-awareness, self-discipline, self-reflection, focus, growth mindset, continuous learning, emotional intelligence, resilience, self-care, positive attitude, adaptability, and purpose & meaning.

SELF-MASTERY CONSISTS OF 12 ELEMENTS

Let's look at the key elements involved in self-mastery.

The 1st key element is **self-awareness**. To accomplish this, you must examine yourself objectively and recognize your abilities, limitations, principles, and convictions. It also consists of understanding your emotions and managing them effectively. Without self-awareness, it's impossible to make positive changes in your life.

The 2nd key element is **self-discipline**. Again, developing the necessary behaviors for success is crucial for achieving and maintaining your objectives in the long run. But, again, it's about being consistent and committed to the actions that will bring you closer to your dreams.

The 3rd key element is **self-reflection**. Reflecting on actions, thoughts, and emotions is crucial to this process. Learning from errors, enhancing conduct, and building self-awareness are benefits of this.

The 4th key element is **focus**. Setting clear objectives and organizing your time and energy in order of importance is part of this process. But, again, it's about saying "no" to distractions and other things that don't align with your goals.

The 5th key element is a **growth mindset**. Embracing challenges as chances for growth and gaining insights from errors is essential to this process. It's about having a positive attitude towards failure and setbacks and using them as steppingstones toward success.

The 6th key element is **continuous learning**. Self-mastery is a lifelong journey of constant learning. It would help if you were open to new ideas, experiences, and perspectives. Growing, evolving, and adapting to changes in your environment are possible outcomes of this process.

The 7th key element is **emotional intelligence**. It is the ability to recognize, understand, and manage your own emotions, as well as the feelings of others.

The 8th key element is **resilience**. It is the ability to bounce back from setbacks and persevere through challenges.

The 9th key element is **self-care**. It is the ability to take care of your physical, mental, and emotional well-being through exercise, healthy eating, meditation, and stress management.

The 10th key element is a **positive attitude**. It is the ability to maintain a positive outlook and focus on the good things in life.

The 11th key element is **adaptability**. It is the ability to adjust to changes and new situations and be open to new ideas and perspectives.

The 12th key element is **purpose and meaning**. It is having a clear sense of purpose and direction in life and aligning your actions with your values and beliefs.

Now, let's look at examples of individuals who have achieved self-mastery. One of my favorite examples is Elon Musk, the CEO of Tesla and SpaceX. He has demonstrated incredible self-mastery by setting audacious goals and pursuing them relentlessly. As a result, he has overcome numerous setbacks and obstacles but has never given up on his dreams. Instead, his focus, discipline, and growth mindset have allowed his extraordinary success.

Another example is Oprah Winfrey, who overcame incredible adversity to become one of the world's most successful and influential women. She has demonstrated remarkable self-awareness by understanding and using her experiences to help others. In addition, her discipline and focus have allowed her to build a media empire and positively impact countless lives.

Self-mastery is the key to living a fulfilling and purposeful life. It involves developing self-awareness, discipline, focus, and a growth mindset. By mastering these key elements, you can achieve anything you want. So, take the time to develop these skills and habits and become the master of your destiny. Remember, you have the power to create the life you want, so go out there and make it happen!

Strategies for Developing Self-Awareness

Are you stuck in a rut, wondering where you're headed? Are you tired of going through the motions without purpose or fulfillment? According to the legendary Dr. Wayne Dyer, the key to breaking free from this cycle and living a life of authenticity, joy, and purpose lies in developing self-awareness. But this isn't just about surface-level introspection - it requires a deep commitment to confronting our fears, doubts, and limiting beliefs. Only then can we build a foundation for personal growth and fulfillment to serve us for a lifetime. So, are you ready to take the first step toward a more meaningful life? Again, it all starts with self-awareness.

One powerful strategy for cultivating self-awareness is to practice mindfulness. By being present in the moment and observing our thoughts and emotions without judgment, we can gain insight into our inner world and better understand our behavior patterns. For example, we tend to react with anger or defensiveness in certain situations. In that case, we can begin to explore the underlying reasons for this and work on developing more constructive responses.

Another practical approach to self-awareness is to seek feedback from others. Seeking feedback from others is a practical approach to self-awareness. It involves being open to constructive criticism and looking honestly at ourselves. Through this process, we can better understand our strengths and weaknesses, allowing us to make positive changes and grow as individuals. However, by inviting honest feedback from people we trust, we can gain a more accurate view of ourselves and identify areas where we can improve. For example, suppose a friend or colleague tells us we tend to interrupt others in conversations. In that case, we can work on listening more actively and giving others space to speak.

Developing self-awareness is a lifelong process that requires ongoing effort and dedication. But by embracing this journey with an open heart and a willingness to learn, we can cultivate a deep sense of self-knowledge and self-acceptance that allows us to live with greater purpose, authenticity, and joy.

Strategies for Developing Self-Discipline

To win the battle of life, you must develop severe self-discipline. It's the key to achieving your goals and becoming the best version of yourself. But it's going to take a lot of work. Self-discipline requires hard work, dedication, and an unwavering commitment to your objectives. So, how can you develop this essential trait?

First off, you need to create a plan and stick to it. I have many different plans in my life that I like to call battle plans. One plan is my financial battle plan, which is my budget. I ensure that every dollar is accounted for by telling my money what to do on paper. I have two different categories one for when I am working and another if I am not. You must plan for every situation that might occur.

Another essential plan is my optimal performance plan, which helps me get the most out of my time and body and leave a lasting impact on the world. My optimal performance plan is a holistic approach to personal growth and development that focuses on achieving one's goals and priorities while optimizing physical and mental performance. It involves managing time effectively, prioritizing physical health, investing in mental wellness, committing to personal growth, embracing biohacking, focusing on recovery, brain hacking for peak performance, and leaving a positive mark on the world. By following this plan, individuals can enhance their overall well-being and achieve their full potential. These are all essential elements to become the best version of yourself for your employer, family, friends, and partner.

Whatever plan you create, live by this word: **No more excuses or procrastination.** If you set a goal, make a detailed plan on how to achieve it and commit to following through. For instance, if you aim to get in shape, create a workout schedule and stick to it, even when you don't feel like it. Avoid making excuses or procrastinating, and always push yourself to stay on track.

Secondly, prioritize your time and energy toward what matters most. Identifying and focusing on your most important tasks precisely is crucial for success in any area of life. Doing so will avoid getting sidetracked by less critical lessons that can consume your time and energy and instead direct your efforts toward your most significant priorities.

One way to prioritize your time is to list all your tasks and rank them in order of importance. Start with the most critical tasks that require immediate attention and work your way down to the less critical ones. For instance, if you're a student, prioritize studying for your upcoming exams over attending social events or leisure activities that can wait until later.

Another way to prioritize your energy is to identify your peak productivity times and allocate your most challenging tasks during these periods. For example, if you're a morning person, use that time to tackle the most demanding tasks that require more concentration and focus. Conversely, if you prefer staying up at night, work on essential tasks you will complete by the next day during the evenings.

Moreover, you can prioritize your energy by minimizing your time on low-value activities such as scrolling through social media or binge-watching TV shows. Instead, use that time to work on your goals or engage in activities that align with your priorities.

Thirdly, hold yourself accountable. Don't make excuses for your mistakes or failures. It's about taking full responsibility for everything in your life, good or bad. To grow and improve, taking ownership of and learning from your mistakes is essential. Blaming others or making excuses won't help, so it's important to accept responsibility for your actions and use your mistakes as opportunities for growth.

It would be best to analyze what went wrong when you missed a workout or failed to meet a goal. It's not the time to beat yourself up over a mistake, but rather an opportunity for reflection and learning. Instead, ask yourself questions like "Why did I miss this workout?" or "What can I do differently to ensure I achieve my goal next time?" This type of self-reflection can help you identify areas for improvement and take the necessary steps to get back on track.

One of the most important things to remember is that taking responsibility for your actions can be challenging. It requires honesty, humility, and a willingness to admit your mistakes. However, it is the hallmark of a disciplined life. When you take responsibility for everything that happens, you become the master of your destiny. You're no longer at the mercy of outside forces or circumstances beyond your control. You're in charge, and you can create the life you want.

Fourthly, practice delayed gratification to build the ability to resist immediate temptation in favor of long-term goals and benefits. As an athlete, I know this all too well; instead of going out and being social, I would stay home and go to bed early because I had to train or compete the next day. Sleep and recovery were more important to me than being social. This reminds me of the famous Marshmallow Experiment, a prime example of the power of delayed gratification in action.

In the experiment, children were offered a marshmallow and told that if they could resist eating it for a certain amount of time, they would receive a second marshmallow as a reward. The researchers found that the children who could delay their gratification and wait for the second marshmallow tended to have better outcomes later in life, including higher academic achievement and better social skills.

To apply this concept to your life, start by identifying areas where you tend to give in to immediate gratification instead of working towards long-term goals. This could be anything from binge-watching TV instead of studying for a test, eating junk food instead of cooking a healthy meal, or spending money on unnecessary purchases instead of saving for the future.

Once you have identified these areas, practice delaying gratification by setting small goals for yourself. For example, if you tend to procrastinate on studying, try setting a timer for 25 minutes and working on your studies without any distractions during that time. After the 25 minutes are up, allow yourself a short break before returning to your studies.

Another way to practice delayed gratification is to break down larger goals into smaller, more manageable tasks. This can help you stay motivated and focused on the long-term benefits of your actions. For example, if you are trying to save money for a big purchase, create a budget and set aside a small amount each week instead of spending all your money at once.

By practicing delayed gratification, you can build your self-control and avoid impulsive behavior that may undermine your goals. With time and practice, you can learn to prioritize long-term benefits over immediate gratification and achieve tremendous success in all areas of your life.

Finally, embracing the struggle and overcoming obstacles in your path toward success is essential. One of the best pieces of advice on this comes from a Navy Seal athlete I trained in the sport of Olympic lifting. He told me to "embrace the suck."

This means acknowledging that the path to success can be challenging, and there will be challenges along the way. However, rather than trying to avoid or ignore these difficulties, facing them head-on and pushing through them is essential. Doing so will develop resilience and determination, which are vital for achieving your goals.

Here are some additional strategies to help you build your self-discipline muscles:

- **Start Small:** Try to keep everything the same. Instead, start with small changes and gradually move to bigger ones. For example, if you want to start exercising regularly, don't commit to an intense workout regimen right away. Instead, start with a 15-minute walk daily and gradually increase the time and intensity.
- **Reward Yourself:** Set up a system of rewards to keep yourself motivated. For example, if you stick to your weekly workout schedule, treat yourself to a movie or a favorite meal. Celebrate your successes, no matter how small.
- **Practice Mindfulness:** Mindfulness is being present at the moment and fully engaged in what you're doing. It can help you stay focused and avoid distractions. Try practicing mindfulness while working on a task, exercising, or even doing household chores.
- **Find an Accountability Partner:** Having someone to hold you accountable can be a powerful motivator. Find a friend or family member who shares your goals and holds each other responsible. Check-in regularly and offer support and encouragement.
- **Use Visualization Techniques:** Visualize yourself succeeding in your goals and achieving your dreams. Use positive

affirmations and imagine yourself already achieving your goals. This can help you stay focused and motivated.

- **Stay Flexible:** It's important to be flexible and willing to adjust your plans as needed. Life is unpredictable, and sometimes things don't go according to plan. So be ready to make adjustments and keep moving forward.

Self-discipline is not an easy trait to develop, but it's critical if you want to succeed in life. Self-discipline takes hard work, dedication, and commitment, but it's ultimately worth it. With these strategies in your toolkit, you can only achieve something.

Strategies for Developing Self-Reflection

Self-reflection is introspecting and examining one's thoughts, emotions, and behaviors. It is an essential tool for personal growth and development. Individuals must gain insight into their true selves and make positive life changes. By reflecting on our experiences, we can better understand our motivations, fears, and desires. Reflection can improve our decision-making and help us lead a more fulfilling life. Self-reflection also allows us to recognize patterns in our thoughts and behaviors, which can help us to identify areas where we need to make changes. When we take responsibility for our own lives and use self-reflection as personal empowerment, we can gain greater clarity about our goals and aspirations and take steps towards achieving them.

The True Nature of Self-Reflection

Self-reflection is not solely about assessing our past actions and making judgments. Instead, it involves looking deeply into our inner selves and observing our thoughts and emotions in the present moment with curiosity and compassion. Through self-reflection, we can gain a more profound insight into our true nature and develop a greater sense of compassion and understanding. In addition, this practice allows us to detach from our ego-driven impulses and cultivate a more mindful and intentional approach to our actions and decisions.

Cultivating a sense of detachment from our ego-driven impulses can be a challenging but transformative process. By letting go of our attachment to our desires and expectations, we can see the world and ourselves more clearly. When you let go of what no longer serves you, you create the space and energy for new and better opportunities to enter your life. By releasing our attachment to our ego-driven impulses, we create the space for inner peace and a deeper understanding of ourselves.

Developing Mindfulness and Intentionality

Developing mindfulness and intentionality can transform your life in ways you never thought possible. When we cultivate mindfulness, we become more aware of our thoughts, feelings, and actions. We learn to live in the present rather than getting lost in worries about the future or regrets about the past. We can be more intentional with our choices and make decisions that align with our values and goals.

Mindfulness can help us to overcome negative emotions and cultivate inner peace. By being intentional with our thoughts and actions, we can create positive change in our lives and the world around us.

For example, when we practice mindfulness and intentionality in our relationships, we can build deeper connections and show our loved ones that they are genuinely valued. When we approach our work intentionally, we can focus on the tasks that matter most and achieve tremendous success. By living mindfully and purposefully, we can find true happiness and live a meaningful life.

Benefits of Self-Reflection

I am a firm believer in the power of self-reflection. It is a practice that allows you to take control of your life and create a genuinely fulfilling future. Through self-reflection, you can better understand yourself, develop greater empathy for others, and enhance your personal growth and development. I will share the incredible benefits of self-reflection that can lead you to live a life of purpose and passion. So, let's dive in and discover how self-reflection can change your life!

Reflecting on our thoughts, feelings, and actions can grant us a deeper understanding of our true nature. Doing so makes us more aware of our strengths, weaknesses, values, and beliefs. This understanding empowers us to focus on our strengths and overcome our weaknesses to live a life of virtue and wisdom. Therefore, let us strive to know ourselves better, as this knowledge enables us to thrive and flourish in accordance with reason.

Through reflecting on our own experiences and emotions, we can cultivate an understanding and appreciation of the experiences and emotions of others. Furthermore, heightened empathy allows us to see the world from multiple perspectives, which leads to improved relationships and a more harmonious society. Therefore, let us practice empathy and strive to understand and respect the views of others, as we are all connected by our shared humanity.

I learned from stoic philosophy that self-reflection can be a powerful tool for improving relationships with others. By reflecting on our biases, triggers, and communication styles, we can better understand ourselves and become more attuned to our thoughts, feelings, and behaviors. Likewise, reflecting on our preferences, motivations, and communication styles can enable us to understand ourselves better, allowing us to become more attuned to our thoughts, feelings, and behaviors. So, let us strive to use self-reflection to improve our relationships with others, recognizing that true wisdom comes from mastering the art of human connection.

Lastly, self-reflection is critical to enhancing personal growth and development. Through reflection, we can set goals, track our progress, and identify areas for improvement. This process enables us to become the best version of ourselves, constantly striving to improve and grow in wisdom and virtue. May we embrace self-reflection as a path to personal excellence and may our pursuit of growth and development be fueled by our commitment to living following our truth.

Through the lens of Stoic philosophy, I have realized the transformative power of self-reflection. By examining my thoughts, feelings, and actions, I have identified my strengths and weaknesses and cultivated a deeper understanding of myself. Through this ongoing practice of self-reflection, I have learned to control my emotions, focus on what I can control, and accept what I cannot.

In embracing this philosophy, I have recognized that pursuing self-knowledge is a lifelong journey requiring constant reflection and self-improvement. By acknowledging my limitations and seeking to grow beyond them, I can live a more meaningful and fulfilling life in accordance with my true nature as a rational being. As such, I will continue to embrace the practice of self-reflection, knowing that it is a path toward personal growth and a life well-lived.

How to Practice Self-Reflection

In pursuing self-reflection, it is crucial to carve out dedicated time for introspection. Just as a master painter carefully set up their canvas and gather their brushes before creating a masterpiece, we too must set aside a sacred space for self-reflection. This might involve finding a peaceful area in a park or establishing a calm environment at home. To allow our thoughts and feelings to surface and lead us to a better level of self-awareness, we can use techniques like meditation, writing, or sitting in silence during this time.

We can improve our understanding by getting input from reliable people. We can ask friends, mentors, or family members for feedback, much like a sculptor does with their fellow artists. By respectfully opening ourselves to others' viewpoints, we obtain new ideas and identify potential blind spots. Their comments serve as a mirror, showing our assets, liabilities, and room for improvement. By engaging in this process of constructive criticism, we can improve our understanding of who we are and the direction we should go.

An important part of self-reflection is accepting difficulties and failures as chances for improvement. Setbacks can be demoralizing because life frequently tosses curveballs at us. However, they also give us wonderful opportunities to grow and develop. Challenges force us to stretch past our comfort zones like a seed buried beneath the earth battling to break free and strive for the sun. We can learn important lessons from them and develop our capacity for tenacity, flexibility, and resilience. Setbacks can be turned into catalysts for development and change by being reframed as stepping-stones on our path.

Being the captain of your ship is a powerful metaphor for the discipline of self-reflection since you are navigating the vast ocean of life. You must frequently review your navigational charts and alter your route to match your intended destination if you want to sail without incident. Similarly, self-reflection enables you to reevaluate your life's course and ensure you remain faithful to your goals and ideals. You develop the skills of a seasoned captain by reflecting, getting feedback, and embracing difficulties, guiding your ship toward a meaningful and satisfying existence.

Think about the penicillin discovery legend of Alexander Fleming. He found a petri dish filled with bacteria when he returned from vacation. Most scientists would have rejected it and written it off as a failure. But instead, he investigated further. The plate had been tainted by a mold, leaving a ring of space around it so that the bacteria could not increase, as his quick inspection had revealed. The invention of antibiotics was facilitated by this unintentional discovery, which radically altered modern medicine. Fleming is an excellent example of how self-reflection may lead to unexpected possibilities because of his capacity to see failures as opportunities for improvement and to reflect on unexpected results.

Dr. Wayne Dyer, one of my many mentors, once said: "When you change the way you look at things, the things you look at change." We allow ourselves to experience great personal transformation by contemplating, asking for feedback from others, and viewing setbacks as chances for growth. We embarked on a transformative journey by adopting this perspective and proactively engaging in self-reflection and kept improving.

Strategies for Developing Focus

You can succeed in any area of your life by concentrating all your mental and physical energy on one activity or goal. So how do you focus like a laser and produce amazing results? Allow me to impart some effective tactics to you.

You must first and foremost have a distinct idea of what you hope to accomplish. Setting precise, quantifiable, and consistent objectives with your values and aspirations is necessary. You're more likely to remain motivated and focused even in the face of distractions or other challenges if you clearly know what you want to accomplish.

Eliminating distractions and creating an environment that supports your goals are two more crucial methods for improving focus. To achieve this, one must eliminate social media and television distractions and designate a workspace that encourages productivity. When you remove distractions and establish a setting that supports your objectives, you're more likely to remain concentrated and productive.

It is crucial to practice mindfulness exercises and cultivate present-moment awareness. It's important to emphasize the need to focus on one task at a time and avoid multitasking. You're more likely to create a flow state, where you're absorbed in the activity at hand and performing at your best when you practice mindfulness and remain in the present moment.

So, my friend, if you want to achieve fantastic results and acquire laser-like focus, it's time to establish a clear vision of what you want to do, get rid of distractions, build an environment that supports your goals, engage in mindfulness practices, and develop a sense of presence in the present. Remember that focus is the key to success in any aspect of your life. With the correct mindset and approaches, you may achieve extraordinary achievements. So, let's put it into action!

Strategies for Developing a Growth Mindset

Are you tired of feeling stuck and held back by limiting beliefs? Are you ready to break free and unleash your full potential? Then developing a growth mindset is essential for you! With a growth mindset, you firmly believe that hard work, persistence, and learning from mistakes can build your abilities and intelligence. It's not just a belief but a powerful mindset that can help you unlock your full potential and achieve great success in life. It's not just a new way of thinking but a new way of life to help you achieve your goals and fulfill your true potential. So, let go of those limiting beliefs and embrace the power of a growth mindset today!

To cultivate a growth mindset:

1. Start by embracing challenges as opportunities for growth.
2. Instead of shying away from complex tasks, approach them with a willingness to learn and improve.

3. Don't let setbacks or failures discourage you; use them as a chance to learn and grow.
4. Remember, mistakes are not failures but rather opportunities to learn and improve.

Next, focus on your efforts and progress rather than just the result. Celebrate your small wins and acknowledge the progress you make towards your goals. Recognize that growth and development take time, so be patient and focus on the process.

Finally, it's essential to seek out feedback and learn from others. Being open to constructive criticism and seeking out mentors and role models who can help you learn, and grow is essential for personal and professional development. When you seek feedback and learn from others, you can continuously improve your skills and knowledge and become more effective and successful.

Developing a growth mindset is a journey that requires effort, persistence, and dedication. However, you can change and develop your abilities over time. With the right attitude and strategies, you can achieve extraordinary success. So, don't limit yourself with negative self-talk or limiting beliefs. Instead, focus on cultivating a growth mindset and see how far you can go! Remember, a growth mindset is critical to achieving your goals and fulfilling your potential. With the right attitude and strategies, you can achieve incredible success. So, let's make it happen!

Strategies for Developing Continuous Learning

Continuous learning is essential for personal growth and success in both personal and professional aspects of life. It is the key to unlocking new opportunities and staying relevant in an ever-changing world. Let me share some strategies to help you develop a lifelong love of learning and keep you motivated to grow.

Firstly, set specific learning goals. Identify what you want to learn and why you want to learn it. For example, you could learn a new language or take up a new hobby. A clear goal will assist you in staying focused and motivated to keep learning.

Secondly, be open to new experiences. Step out of your comfort zone and experience something new. For example, take a class in a subject you've always been interested in, or attend a workshop on a skill you've always wanted to develop. Embrace the newness and learn as much as you can from experience.

Thirdly, is to seek out mentors and role models. Finding individuals who have achieved your desired success and learning from their experiences and insights is essential. For example, you might read books or attend events by successful entrepreneurs or leaders in your industry.

Finally, making learning a part of your daily routine is essential. Setting aside time daily or weekly to engage in learning activities such as reading, listening to podcasts, taking courses, or other similar activities is crucial. When you prioritize learning, you can continuously expand your knowledge and skills and stay ahead of the curve in your field.

Remember that you have the power to shape your future and create a life that is rich with learning and personal growth. By setting specific learning goals, being open to new experiences, and seeking feedback and mentorship, you can keep yourself motivated and engaged in the learning process. So, let's embrace the joy of learning and make it a lifelong pursuit. With the right mindset and strategies, you can cultivate a lifelong love of learning and achieve incredible success. So, let's make it happen!

Strategies for Developing Emotional Intelligence

Developing emotional intelligence is a crucial step in becoming a more self-aware and empathetic individual. Moreover, it is the key to building healthy relationships in our personal and professional lives. So, let me share some strategies to help you develop your emotional intelligence and unlock your true potential.

First and foremost, you need to become more aware of your emotions. Recognizing and labeling your feelings and understanding how they influence your thoughts and behaviors is critical to developing emotional intelligence. When you become more aware of your feelings, you can better regulate them and make more conscious decisions. For example, let's say you're feeling angry about something at work. Take a moment to ask yourself why you're feeling angry. Is it because you feel undervalued or disrespected? Once you have identified the root cause, you can work towards addressing the issue.

Secondly, practicing active listening and empathy is another critical strategy for developing emotional intelligence. Being fully present and engaged when communicating and seeking to understand the person's perspectives and emotions is crucial for developing emotional intelligence. For example, you might try to put yourself in their shoes and imagine how they might be feeling to understand their perspective. Practicing empathy and understanding others' perspectives and emotions will help you communicate better and build stronger relationships. For instance, another example is if a friend is upset, instead of telling them to "get over it," try to understand what they're going through and offer support.

Thirdly, learn to manage your stress effectively. Stress can affect your emotional well-being, so it's essential to have healthy coping mechanisms in place. Engaging in activities such as exercise, meditation, or spending time in nature can help you manage your stress effectively.

Finally, it's vital to practice self-reflection and seek feedback from others. Reflecting on your actions and behaviors and seeking input from trusted friends or mentors are essential in developing emotional intelligence. When you are open to feedback and willing to make changes, you can continuously improve your emotional intelligence and become a more effective communicator and leader.

Cultivating emotional intelligence is a journey that requires dedication and persistence. But by regularly reflecting on your emotions, practicing empathy, and managing your stress, you'll become more self-aware and empathetic. And this, in turn, will lead to more fulfilling relationships and a happier life. So, remember, my friend, you can shape your emotional intelligence and, ultimately, your destiny.

Strategies for Building Resilience

In today's fast-paced and ever-changing world, resilience has become an essential quality to possess. Resilience means returning from setbacks, adapting to changes, and moving forward. It involves facing challenges with strength and flexibility and learning from experiences instead of being defeated. Resilience is not an innate trait; it's a mindset and a set of abilities that can be honed through practice and intentional effort.

We will look at some practical methods for developing resilience that can assist you in overcoming obstacles and thriving in the face of difficulty. You can strengthen your resilience and accomplish your goals by using these techniques, regardless of the challenges you face.

- **Cultivate a Positive Mindset:** This strategy involves focusing on the positive aspects of your life and staying optimistic, even in challenging situations. For example, if you're facing a challenging work project, focus on your skills and experience that can help you tackle the task. Instead of feeling overwhelmed, approach the project with a positive attitude and the belief that you can complete it successfully.

- **Build a Strong Support System:** Building a solid support system can involve finding a mentor or coach who can help guide you through difficult times. For example, suppose you're an entrepreneur facing challenges in growing your business. In that case, you can seek a mentor with experience in your industry. This mentor can provide guidance, encouragement, and a fresh perspective.

- **Practice Self-Care:** Self-care involves caring for your physical and emotional needs, which can help you build the resilience you need to face challenges. For example, if you're feeling stressed or overwhelmed, taking a break to relax, such as reading a book or walking, can help you recharge your batteries and feel more resilient.

- **Develop Coping Skills:** Developing coping skills can help you manage stress and regulate your emotions, which are crucial for building resilience. For example, practicing deep breathing exercises can assist to calm your mind and reducing stress levels if you're feeling anxious or overwhelmed. Similarly, taking a break to run or engage in another physical activity can help you healthily release your emotions if you're angry or frustrated.

- **Focus on Growth and Learning:** Focusing on growth and learning involves viewing challenges as opportunities for personal and professional development. For example, if you've experienced a setback in your career, such as losing a job or missing out on a promotion, focus on what you can learn from the experience. Use the setback to develop new skills, improve your performance, and position yourself for future success.

- **Develop a Growth Mindset:** A growth mindset sees challenges as opportunities for learning and growing. Instead of viewing challenges as roadblocks, see them as chances to develop your skills and become a stronger, more capable person. Implementing this can enhance your ability to bounce back and adjust to new situations faster.
- **Take Action:** Taking action is an essential strategy for building resilience. When facing a challenge, it's easy to feel overwhelmed or stuck. However, taking action can help you feel more in control and build confidence, even if it's a small step. For example, if you're facing a challenging project at work, breaking it down into smaller tasks and completing one task at a time can help you progress and feel more resilient.
- **Develop a Sense of Purpose:** A sense of purpose can help you build resilience and stay motivated, even in difficult times. Identify your values and goals and use them as a guide for making decisions and taking action. For example, if you're an environmental activist, your purpose may be to protect the planet and advocate for sustainability. This purpose can help you stay resilient and focused, even when facing challenges.

Building resilience is a lifelong process that requires effort and dedication. However, by practicing these strategies, you can develop your resilience and become more capable of facing challenges and achieving your goals.

Overcoming Adversity and Challenges

Overcoming adversity and challenges is a crucial aspect of our spiritual training, as it helps us to develop our inner strength and resilience. In this topic, I will share insights on overcoming obstacles and emerging stronger from life's challenges.

One of the fundamental teachings in Buddhism I learned is impermanence, which means that everything is in a constant state of flux, and nothing lasts forever. Therefore, challenges are inevitable, and we must develop the right mindset and skills to navigate them. The first step is to accept that challenges are a part of life and that we cannot control everything. We can only control our response to the situation.

One of the strategies to overcome adversity is to cultivate inner peace and calmness. By training our minds to be present at the moment and not be caught up in the past or future, we can reduce the impact of external stressors. One can attain inner peace through meditation, mindfulness, and contemplation. By achieving inner peace, individuals can face challenges with clarity and calmness.

Another strategy is to develop a positive attitude and outlook toward life. Instead of focusing on the situation's negative aspects, we can look for the silver lining and find opportunities for growth and learning. For example, during the COVID-19 pandemic, many people faced financial hardships and job losses. However, some individuals used this as an opportunity to pursue their passion, learn new skills, or start their own business.

Another example of overcoming adversity is J.K. Rowling, author of the Harry Potter series. Before her success, Rowling faced multiple rejections from publishers and was a single mother on welfare. However, she pursued her passion for writing, and her perseverance paid off. Today, she is one of the most successful authors of all time, with her books selling over 500 million copies worldwide. Her story is a testament to the power of resilience and determination in adversity.

Sylvester Stallone is another inspiring example of overcoming adversity. At the beginning of his career, Stallone faced difficulties with acting due to his appearance and speech impediment, which frequently caused him to be rejected for roles. However, he never gave up on his dream and continued to write and submit screenplays. Despite being repeatedly rejected, he persevered and eventually sold the script for the movie Rocky, which went on to win three Academy Awards, including Best Picture.

Getting Rocky made was an uphill battle in itself. Stallone was initially offered a large sum of money for the rights to the screenplay but refused to sell it unless he was cast in the lead role. This led to a long and challenging negotiation process, as studios hesitated to cast an unknown actor in a leading role. Eventually, Stallone was allowed to star in the film, and the rest is history.

Stallone's story demonstrates the importance of never giving up on your dreams, no matter how challenging the circumstances. Through hard work, persistence, and resilience, he overcame the odds and achieved his goals.

If you're unfamiliar with the tale of Rocky, let me fill you in. Rocky Balboa is a fictional character from the movie Rocky who is an excellent example of overcoming adversity. Rocky is an amateur boxer from Philadelphia who gets the chance of a lifetime when he is selected to fight the heavyweight champion of the world, Apollo Creed. Despite being an underdog and facing seemingly insurmountable odds, Rocky trains relentlessly and always keeps sight of his goal. He uses his determination, grit, and resilience to overcome challenges and setbacks throughout his training and the fight. In the end, Rocky becomes a champion not just in the ring but also in life. His story shows that anyone can overcome adversity and achieve their dreams with hard work, perseverance, and a never-give-up attitude.

Finally, it is essential to seek support from others when facing challenges. This could be from friends, family, or professionals like therapists or spiritual teachers. We can gain new perspectives and insights and receive practical support by opening up and sharing our struggles with others.

Overcoming adversity and challenges is an ongoing process that requires us to cultivate inner strength and resilience. By accepting challenges as a part of life, growing inner peace and calmness, developing a positive attitude, and seeking support from others, we can emerge stronger and wiser from life's challenges. Remember, challenges are not setbacks but rather opportunities to grow and evolve.

Finally, knowing how to overcome adversity and challenges on your journey toward building resilience is essential. Adversity can come in many forms, such as job loss, health issues, or relationship problems. Focusing on your strengths and finding solutions to issues is critical to overcoming adversity. This might involve seeking out resources, taking action toward your goals, or seeking support from others.

Remember, building resilience is a process that requires intentional effort and practice. But by focusing on the definition of resilience, developing strategies to enhance it, and overcoming adversity and challenges, you can cultivate the strength and flexibility needed to achieve your goals and create a fulfilling life.

Strategies for Practicing Self-Care

Self-care is essential for maintaining your physical, emotional, and mental health and is critical to living a fulfilling life. So, how can you prioritize self-care and create a healthy, sustainable lifestyle? Let me share with you some powerful strategies.

First and foremost, you need to make self-care a non-negotiable priority in your life. This means recognizing that self-care is not selfish, but rather it's essential for your well-being. When you prioritize self-care, you are better equipped to handle stress and challenges and show up as your best self in all areas of your life.

Another critical strategy for practicing self-care is to create healthy habits and routines. This means incorporating daily activities that nourish your mind, body, and soul. For example, you might start your day with a morning meditation or yoga practice, take regular breaks to stretch and move your body, and wind down with a relaxing bath or book before bed.

Finally, it's essential to be intentional with your time and energy. This means setting boundaries and saying no to things that don't align with your values or goals. When you are intentional with your time and energy, you can prioritize the things that matter most to you and create a balance in your life.

Suppose you want to prioritize self-care and create a healthy, sustainable lifestyle. In that case, it's time to make self-care a non-negotiable priority, develop healthy habits and routines, and be intentional with your time and energy. Remember, self-care is essential for your well-being. By prioritizing it, you can live a fulfilling and purposeful life. So, let's make it happen!

Strategies for Developing a Positive Attitude

It's important to maintain a positive outlook if you want to achieve happiness and success. Let's discuss why. How you approach life significantly impacts your perspective and ability to achieve your goals and find happiness. How can you cultivate a positive outlook that enables you to flourish? Let me provide you with some helpful and motivating tips.

Cultivating thankfulness is the first step in creating a positive attitude. Every day, reflect on and be grateful for your blessings. You will start focusing more on the positive aspects of your life, which will divert your attention from the negative ones. Being thankful makes it easier to appreciate the beauty and goodness around you. It enhances your life's sense of calm and joy.

Another critical strategy for developing a positive attitude is to focus on solutions rather than problems. Instead of dwelling on the negative situation, focus on finding solutions and taking action to produce a better outcome. Gaining control and empowerment over your circumstances can help you adopt a problem-solving mindset.

To make your journey towards positivity even more compelling:

1. Seek inspiration from others who have overcome adversity with a positive attitude.
2. Read books, watch interviews, and attend conferences.
3. Surround yourself with individuals who radiate positivity and learn from their experiences.
4. Remember, your attitude is contagious, and the people around you will be affected by your mindset.

Let me give you an example of someone who has developed a remarkable positive attitude. Nick Vujicic, born without arms and legs, has become a renowned motivational speaker and author. Instead of dwelling on his disabilities, Nick focused on his strengths and pursued his passions, inspiring millions worldwide with his positive attitude and indomitable spirit.

Developing a positive attitude is a journey that requires cultivating gratitude, focusing on solutions, and seeking inspiration from others. With a positive attitude, you can overcome adversity, achieve your goals, and live a fulfilling and successful life. Remember, your attitude is your greatest asset, and with the right mindset, anything is possible.

Strategies for Developing Adaptability

I want to talk to you about one of the most important skills you can develop in today's rapidly changing world: adaptability. Life is unpredictable, and adapting to new situations and challenges is essential for success and happiness. So, how can you develop your adaptability and thrive in any circumstance? Let me share with you some powerful strategies.

The first step in developing adaptability through curiosity is cultivating a mindset of openness and exploration. Be willing to try new things, take risks, embrace uncertainty, and step out of your comfort zone. Instead of fearing the unknown, approach it with curiosity and a desire to learn. Ask questions, seek out new information, and challenge your assumptions. This will expand your knowledge and skills and help you adapt to new situations and challenges.

Another crucial strategy for developing adaptability is to practice flexibility. This means being willing to adjust your plans or approach when circumstances change. To be adaptable, you must pivot quickly and make course corrections as needed. For instance, if unexpected obstacles arise in a project, you might need to revise your timeline or alter your approach to achieve your goals. Being flexible and adaptable allows you to navigate the changing landscape of life with confidence and resilience.

To make your journey towards adaptability even more compelling, find inspiration from others who have embraced curiosity in their lives. Read books, watch interviews, and attend conferences. Seek out individuals who have succeeded through curiosity and learning from their experiences. Additionally, surround yourself with positive, supportive individuals who encourage your curiosity and provide a safe space for exploration and growth.

Let me give you an example of someone who has developed remarkable adaptability through curiosity. Take Elon Musk, for instance. He has built a reputation as one of the world's most innovative and adaptable entrepreneurs. Through his unwavering curiosity and desire to explore new technologies and industries, he has founded several successful companies, including SpaceX and Tesla. Moreover, Elon's passion for learning and exploration has allowed him to adapt to the ever-changing business landscape and stay ahead of the curve.

Developing adaptability through curiosity and practicing flexibility are powerful ways to navigate life's challenges and discover your full potential. It requires cultivating a mindset of openness and exploration, seeking inspiration from others who have embraced curiosity, and surrounding yourself with positive, supportive individuals. With a curious attitude, you can embrace change and uncertainty, discover new opportunities, and adapt to any situation that comes your way.

Strategies for Developing Purpose and Meaning

As humans, we often neglect to contemplate our sense of purpose and meaning, preoccupied with various distractions, leaving us little time to ponder the fundamental questions of our existence: why we are here and how long we have.

Without a clear understanding of direction and a reason for being, it's easy to get lost or stuck in life. So, how can you develop purpose and meaning that genuinely resonates with you? Let me share with you some powerful strategies.

First, you must understand your values and what matters most to you. Then, take the time to reflect on what drives you and what brings you joy. What are your passions and interests? What do you want to contribute to the world? Once you clearly understand what's truly important to you, you can align your life around those values.

Another critical strategy is to set goals that align with your values and purpose. Plans give you something to work towards, and they help you stay motivated and focused. First, however, it's essential to set goals that are meaningful and inspiring to you. For example, suppose your purpose is to help others. In that case, your goals include volunteering at a local shelter, starting a non-profit organization, or becoming a counselor.

Finally, taking action toward your purpose and meaning every day is essential. This might mean taking small steps toward your goals or simply practicing gratitude and mindfulness. When you act towards your purpose, you create momentum and positive energy to help you overcome obstacles and stay committed to your vision.

So, my friend, if you want to live a life full of purpose and meaning, it's time to get clear on your values, set inspiring goals, and act toward your vision daily. Remember, you have the power to create the life you truly desire, and with the right strategies and mindset, you can achieve anything you set your mind to. So, let's make it happen!

Recap: The Importance and Benefits of Self-Mastery

Let's review the incredible benefits and advantages of self-mastery as we proceed on the path to personal greatness, ladies and gentlemen. I want to provide you with the information and mindset needed today so that you may start creating an amazing life.

Self-awareness is the first and most important step toward self-mastery. We may clearly identify who we are by knowing our talents, limitations, values, and beliefs. Self-awareness is the cornerstone of progress because it empowers us to make deliberate decisions and carry out deeds consistent with our true selves.

To truly master ourselves, we must cultivate self-discipline. This trait enables us to resist temptations and diversion and maintain our devotion to our objectives. By exercising self-control, we develop the resilience required to face any obstacles that come our way.

Another essential component of self-mastery is self-reflection. We learn a lot about our ideas, feelings, and behaviors when we take the time to reflect. Through self-reflection, we can spot trends, adjust our course, and develop steadily into the best versions of ourselves.

Focus, my friends, is the laser beam that cuts through the noise and propels us forward. By using the power of focus, we may focus our attention and effort on the most important goals. We can avoid outside distractions, keep our heads clear, and produce amazing outcomes.

The fuel of the growth mindset lights the fire of self-mastery. It's the conviction that effort and hard work can help us improve our skills and intelligence. Adopting a growth mindset allows us to actively seek new information, abilities, and views that will help us reach higher levels of achievement.

Emotional intelligence is an indispensable pillar of self-mastery. We build stronger connections and improve our interpersonal interactions by being aware of, controlling, and comprehending our emotions and those of others. Thanks to emotional intelligence, we may successfully negotiate problems, encourage teamwork, and take on leadership roles in all spheres of life.

Friends, the line of defense between us and life's storms is resilience. It's the ability to move past failures, adjust to change, and continue. We can use resilience to transform setbacks into opportunities for success.

A vital part of self-mastery is physically and mentally caring for oneself. By putting our health first, we restore our vitality, boost our output, and build a solid basis for success. Investing in our overall performance and happiness requires self-care; it is not selfish.

Self-mastery's hidden weapon is an optimistic outlook. By keeping a positive mindset, we attract abundance and start a positive chain reaction in our life. An optimistic outlook gives us the strength to face challenges head-on and encourages others to do the same.

In a world that is changing quickly, self-mastery is characterized by adaptability. We thrive in the face of uncertainty and forge on through unfamiliar territory by embracing flexibility and openness. Being adaptable enables us to take advantage of opportunities, change with the times, and maintain our competitive edge.

Ultimately, self-mastery finds its true purpose and meaning. By aligning our actions with our values and passions, we experience a deep sense of fulfillment. We feel a great feeling of fulfillment when our activities are in line with our beliefs and passions. We acknowledge that our journey is about something bigger than ourselves, and we make a positive difference in our local and global communities.

Thank yourself for starting this life-changing journey toward self-mastery because it is an ongoing process. Embrace emotional intelligence, resilience, self-care, a positive attitude, flexibility, purpose, and meaning. Also, embrace self-awareness, self-discipline, self-reflection, focus, a growth mindset, and constant learning. Utilize these guidelines to help you realize your incredible potential. Keep in mind that you can design the life of your dreams.

Story of Self-Mastery

One of the most inspiring stories of self-mastery belongs to Kobe Bryant, the legendary basketball player who dedicated himself to his craft and became one of the greatest athletes of all time.

Throughout his life, Kobe Bryant was dedicated to mastering himself. He accomplished this by embodying positive attitudes, adaptability, purpose and meaning, self-awareness, self-discipline, self-reflection, focus, a growth mindset, continuous learning, emotional intelligence, resilience, and self-care.

Bryant's journey to self-mastery began when he fell in love with basketball at a young age. He was determined to become the best player and was willing to do whatever it took to achieve that goal. He worked tirelessly on his skills, practicing for hours and studying the game with a keen eye for detail.

Bryant's positive attitude was a critical factor in his success. He believed in himself and his abilities, even when others doubted him. He approached each game and each challenge with a mindset of positivity and resilience, and he refused to let setbacks or failures define him.

Bryant's adaptability was another essential factor in his success. He was able to adjust his game to the changing demands of the sport and always looked for ways to improve and stay ahead of the competition. For example, he famously adopted a post-up game in the latter part of his career to compensate for his declining athleticism.

A deep sense of purpose and meaning drove Bryant's pursuit of self-mastery. He understood that basketball was more than just a game; it was a way to inspire others and positively impact the world. In addition, he was passionate about using his platform to promote social justice and equality, and he was deeply committed to his family and his role as a father.

Bryant's self-awareness was a crucial part of his journey to self-mastery. He was honest about his strengths and weaknesses and always sought feedback from others to help him improve. He was also willing to confront his flaws and work to overcome them, evidenced by his public apology to a woman who accused him of sexual assault in 2003.

Bryant's self-discipline was legendary. He had a strict training regimen that he followed religiously and held himself to a high standard of excellence in everything he did. As a result, he could stay focused on his goals and resist distractions, allowing him to achieve a success that few others have ever achieved.

Bryant's self-reflection was another critical part of his journey to self-mastery. He was constantly analyzing his performance and seeking ways to improve. However, he also took time to reflect on his experiences and use them as learning opportunities to grow and develop.

Bryant's focus was unparalleled. He could block out distractions and stay entirely focused on the task, whether it was a game-winning shot or a conversation with a teammate. He had an uncanny ability to tune out the noise and stay completely present in the moment.

Bryant's growth mindset was another important factor in his journey to self-mastery. He believed he could always improve and was never satisfied with his performance. He always sought new challenges and opportunities to learn and grow, even later in his career.

Bryant's commitment to continuous learning was evident in everything he did. He was an avid reader, constantly seeking new knowledge and perspectives. He also sought mentors and advisors who could help him grow and develop as a person and player.

Bryant's emotional intelligence was a crucial part of his success. He connected with his teammates and coaches on a deep level and was a master at reading the emotions of those around him. He could also control his emotions and remain calm and focused in high-pressure situations.

Finally, Bryant's resilience and self-care were essential to his journey to self-mastery. He faced numerous setbacks and challenges throughout his career, including injuries and personal tragedies. Still, he was always able to bounce back and keep pushing forward. He also recognized the importance of self-care, taking time to rest and recharge to perform at his best.

One of the most inspiring examples of Bryant's self-mastery came in the 2009 NBA Finals. The Los Angeles Lakers faced the Orlando Magic in a tough series that had gone to a decisive Game 5.

Bryant struggled in the previous game, scoring 8 points on 3-of-10 shooting. But instead of dwelling on his poor performance, he came into Game 5 with a positive attitude and a determination to lead his team to victory.

Bryant was unstoppable that night, scoring 30 points and leading the Lakers to a 99-86 victory and his fourth NBA championship. He showed his ability to adapt by changing his game plan to capitalize on the defensive strategies used by the Magic. In addition, he recognized the importance of self-awareness and self-reflection, using his previous performance as motivation to improve.

Throughout his career, Bryant embodied the qualities of self-mastery that he worked so hard to develop. His positive attitude, adaptability, purpose and meaning, self-awareness, self-discipline, self-reflection, focus, growth mindset, continuous learning, emotional intelligence, resilience, and self-care were all essential to his success. And his commitment to self-mastery continues to inspire others to pursue their path to greatness.

Self-Assessment Questions

- What specific goals or outcomes do you aspire to achieve in your personal growth and development?
- Can you identify any limiting beliefs or self-imposed barriers that may be hindering your progress towards self-mastery?
- How do you typically respond to setbacks, challenges, or obstacles? Are there alternative perspectives or approaches that you can adopt to overcome them?
- What strategies or techniques have you found effective in managing your emotions and maintaining a state of resourcefulness in challenging situations?

- Are there any recurring patterns or habits that you would like to change or transform in order to enhance your self-mastery? How can you cultivate new, empowering patterns?
- What are some areas of your life where you feel you have already achieved a significant level of self-mastery? What lessons can you learn from those experiences to apply to other areas?
- How do you leverage your strengths and talents to cultivate self-mastery in different aspects of your life? Are there any untapped strengths that you can further develop?
- How do you approach self-reflection and self-awareness? Are there specific practices or rituals that you find helpful in deepening your understanding of yourself?
- Can you recall a time when you demonstrated resilience and adaptability in the face of change or adversity? How can you draw upon those qualities to continue advancing on your path to self-mastery?
- Reflect on the vision of the person you aspire to become in terms of self-mastery. What steps can you take today to align your thoughts, actions, and beliefs with that vision?

Self-Mastery Action Steps

- **Develop a Growth Mindset:** Self-mastery begins with a growth mindset. This means believing you can develop and improve your abilities through effort and hard work. Embrace challenges as opportunities to learn and grow and cultivate a positive attitude towards yourself and your abilities.
- **Set Clear Goals:** Determine what you want to achieve in your life, such as career, relationships, health, and personal growth. Set specific, measurable goals that align with

your values and vision for your life. Break these goals into smaller, actionable steps you can take daily.

- **Create a Plan:** Develop a plan of action to achieve your goals. Consider the resources, skills, and support you need and potential obstacles and setbacks. Schedule regular checkpoints to assess your progress and adjust your plan as needed.

- **Develop Self-Discipline:** Self-mastery requires self-discipline, which means developing the ability to control your impulses, emotions, and behaviors. Practice self-discipline in small ways, such as setting a regular sleep schedule, avoiding distractions while working, or avoiding unhealthy foods.

- **Practice Mindfulness:** Mindfulness is being fully present and aware in the moment, without judgment or distraction. This can help you develop self-awareness, manage stress, and improve focus and concentration. Incorporate mindfulness practices such as meditation, deep breathing, or yoga into your daily routine.

- **Seek Feedback:** Seek feedback from others who can provide honest and constructive feedback on your progress toward your goals. This can help you identify blind spots and areas for improvement and reinforce positive behaviors and achievements.

- **Learn Continuously:** Self-mastery requires a commitment to lifelong learning and development. Seek opportunities to learn and grow in areas relevant to your goals and interests, such as reading books, attending workshops, or taking courses

Remember, self-mastery is a journey, not a destination. You can achieve self-mastery and live a fulfilling and successful life by taking consistent action toward your goals and committing to lifelong learning and growth.

Self-Mastery Exercises

- **Breath Awareness Meditation:** Take a few minutes daily to sit quietly and focus on your breath. Breathe deeply and slowly and observe the sensation of the air entering and leaving your body. This exercise will help you develop greater awareness and control over your mind and emotions.
- **Gratitude Journaling:** At the end of each day, write down three things you are grateful for. This exercise will help you cultivate a positive outlook and resilience in facing challenges.
- **Digital Detox:** Take a break from your phone and other digital devices for a set period each day. Use this time to connect with yourself and your surroundings and to engage in activities that bring you joy and fulfillment.
- **Mindful Eating:** Pay attention to the eating experience, from the colors and textures of the food to the sensations in your body. Chew your food slowly and savor each bite. This exercise will help you better understand your body and its needs.
- **Visualization:** Take a few minutes each day to visualize yourself succeeding in a particular goal or overcoming a particular challenge. Use all your senses to create a vivid picture of yourself achieving your desired outcome. This exercise will help you build confidence and motivation.

Positive Affirmation

In the pursuit of self-mastery, you become the author of your own narrative. You rewrite the script of your life, empowering yourself to overcome limitations and transcend self-imposed boundaries. You awaken to the truth that you have the power to create your reality, and you wield that power with wisdom and integrity.

ABOUT THE AUTHOR

Frederick is a seasoned expert in high-performance and mental toughness with a wealth of experience and knowledge. He can help lead you on a transformative journey from being the underdog to a champion with his guidance. Frederick will teach you the ways of the inner warrior mindset, helping you eliminate limiting beliefs that may be hindering your success.

Throughout his life, Frederick has been an athlete for over four decades, competing in various sports, including baseball, basketball, football, tennis, powerlifting, weightlifting, body-building, and track. In college, he was a track sprinter at the division one level. His dream of representing the United States in international competitions began after watching the Olympics, and he went on to achieve that dream, representing the U.S. at world cup competitions and the Pan-Americans in the sport of Olympic Weightlifting.

Despite not being the tallest, biggest, fastest, strongest, or smartest athlete and student, Frederick approached every day as an opportunity to improve and learn from his mistakes. He motivates and inspires others to embrace their inner underdog as fuel to become a champion in all areas of life. Frederick is certified in Neuro-Linguistic Programming, high-performance coaching, and sports performance hypnosis, a USA Weightlifting Sports Performance Coach, and a six-sigma green belt certified. He holds a degree in electrical engineering and is the author of "*What The F.R.E.D!: Mastering the Four Essential Traits for an Unstoppable Mindset, "Financial Game Plan for Your Dollars and Cents: A Step-by-Step, Common-Sense Approach to Making the Right Financial Decisions*" and co-author of the international bestseller "*1% More: The Hidden Force to Creating Extraordinary Results in Life & Business.*"

AUTHOR CONTACT INFORMATION

www.FredMartinez.info
www.ThePathIsTheWay.com

ACKNOWLEDGMENTS

I am eternally grateful to the people who taught me the true meaning of unconditional love: my mother, Ramona Martinez; my father, Alejandro "Alex" Martinez II; my brothers, Alex Martinez III and Leroy Martinez; my sisters, Yvonne Diaz, Karen Martinez, and Sharon Martinez. Their love and guidance have been instrumental in shaping who I am today. I am forever in their debt for the sacrifices they made and the endless love they have given me throughout my life. I cannot thank them enough for their profound impact on me and for showing me what true love looks like.

I am deeply grateful to my childhood friends, who played such a significant role in shaping my life. Your presence in my life made my childhood an unforgettable journey of fun and excitement. I will always cherish the memories we shared, big and small, and I am forever grateful for your impact on me. Without our shared experiences, I would not be who I am today. Thank you from the bottom of my heart.

I am deeply grateful to the coaches and mentors who have played a vital role in my journey. Their guidance and encouragement have helped me become who I am today. I am so thankful for the time and effort they invested in me, pushing me to be better than I was yesterday and helping me to reach my full potential. I will always be grateful for the knowledge, skills, and wisdom they have imparted.

ACKNOWLEDGMENTS

Their impact on my life has been immeasurable, and I will always carry their teachings with me. Thank you with heartfelt gratitude.

Lastly, I want to express my deepest gratitude to my teammates. Your unwavering support and camaraderie have been a constant source of inspiration and motivation for me. Your encouragement and push to greatness have helped me to achieve more than I ever thought possible. I am honored to have had the opportunity to work and grow alongside such an amazing group of people. I will always treasure the memories and experiences we shared. Thank you for being my teammates and friends and helping me become the best version of myself.

If you liked this book, please consider leaving us a review. We are truly grateful for every review we receive, as it enables us to expand our reach and connect with a wider audience. Thank you very much!

OTHER WORKS BY FREDERICK A. MARTINEZ

OTHER WORKS BY FREDERICK A. MARTINEZ

Milton Keynes UK
Ingram Content Group UK Ltd.
UKHW030700120324
439302UK00017B/1165